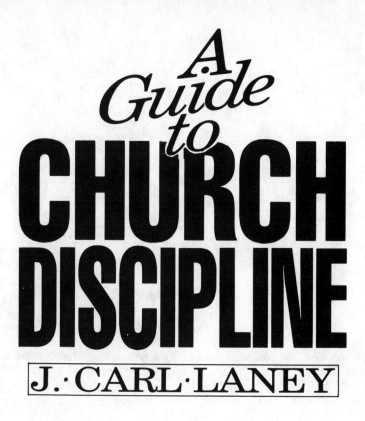

A Guide to CHURCH DISCIPLINE

J. CARL LANEY

BETHANY HOUSE PUBLISHERS
MINNEAPOLIS, MINNESOTA 55438
A Division of Bethany Fellowship, Inc.

Published by Bethany House Publishers
A Division of Bethany Fellowship, Inc.
6820 Auto Club Road, Minneapolis, Minnesota 55438

Printed in the United States of America

Library of Congress Cataloging in Publication Data

Laney, J. Carl, 1948–
   A guide to church discipline.
   Bibliography: p.
   Includes index.
   1. Church discipline.   I. Title.
BV740.L35   1985   262'.8   85-15121
ISBN 0-87123-834-9

ACKNOWLEDGMENTS

This book is the fruit of many laborers. I am indebted to Bethany House Publishers for their interest in this project and for their support in preparing the pastors' survey. Editors Carol Johnson and Nathan Unseth have been particularly helpful in providing me with an unending stream of articles and material related to the subject of church discipline. I am grateful to Drs. Don Smith, Roger Bufford, and Tim Irwin who offered helpful suggestions in the technical development of the survey. Dr. Gerry Breshears graciously provided me with a computer program suitable for collating the data I collected. Carolyn Bublat was indispensable in the work of typing addresses and preparing the envelopes for the mailing. My appreciation extends also to John Laney, my eight-year-old son, who licked the stamps for the survey's 1,250 return envelopes!

Most of all, I owe appreciation to the hundreds of pastors who spent valuable time responding to my survey. Their experiences and insights provide this book's distinctive contribution to the study of church discipline. The data from the survey has enabled me to analyze the truths of God's Word in the context of real life experience. I have been challenged to scrutinize my own viewpoints and to give these chapters a more practical focus. I have sought, therefore, to make this book a practical and biblical guide for confronting and correcting sinning saints.

To the pastors and Christian leaders who are striving to apply the truths of church discipline, I respectfully dedicate this book.

J. Carl Laney

132706

FOREWORD

One cannot read the Scripture, Old or New Testament, without seeing repeatedly that God pursues with zeal the holiness of His people. In 1 Peter 1:16 is a summary of God's desire for those who are called by His name: "Be ye holy; for I am holy" (KJV). Yet if one thing characterizes the contemporary church, it is a lack of integrity in the matter of holiness. While churches affirm the authority of Scripture and identify what is sinful, they utterly fail in the responsibility of enforcing that affirmation in the life of the Body. Evangelicalism has been guilty too long of the gross hypocrisy of fighting for the authority of the Bible and the doctrine of inerrancy, all the while dealing softly with the practical implications of those doctrines.

Early in my ministry, a beloved man of God, who had traversed this country for years and preached in all kinds of churches and Bible conferences, said to me, "I don't know of a single church in the United States of America that is involved in disciplining its sinning members—not one."

Another leading pastor told me, "If you discipline church members, they'll never stand for it, and you'll empty the place. You can't run around sticking your nose into everyone's sin."

That attitude is a reflection of both the fallenness of man and the independent spirit of our age. The prevailing philosophy is, "I'll take care of me, and you take care of you, and we'll get along better that way."

Yet hardly anyone would deny that the contemporary church, though outwardly large and active, is inwardly weak and ineffective. Why? The issue is not that we have preached the wrong message, but rather that we have failed to be obedient in its implementation in the lives of the people. We have said, in effect, "As long as your belief is correct, I don't care how you behave."

But sin must be dealt with. It isn't enough to make announcements or post rules—righteousness must be enforced. As a father must discipline to correct a child, and as a teacher must chasten students to help them learn, so must those who are charged with the spiritual oversight of God's people lovingly correct those who fall short of the pattern of righteousness.

For too long we have misinterpreted Matt. 7:1, "Judge not, that ye be not judged" (KJV), and ignored the admonition of 1 Cor. 11:31, "If we would judge ourselves, we should not be judged" (KJV).

Carl Laney thoughtfully and biblically pleads for a return to the proper practice of corrective church discipline. His message is one which pastors, church leaders, and church members can no longer brush aside. The contemporary church is faltering, threatened more by impurity from within than by persecution from without. Its health, testimony, and usefulness for the Lord are at stake. To help restore her to the position of holiness to which God called her, we must obey Christ's call to His church: discipline. It must become a crucial part of the ministry, a responsibility we cannot neglect if our obedience is to be complete.

John MacArthur, Jr.
Pastor, Grace Community
Church

CONTENTS

INTRODUCTION

The *Belgic Confession* (1561), which grew out of Reformation soil, identifies three characteristics "by which the true church is known." These marks are: (1) the preaching of pure doctrine, (2) the administering of the sacraments, and (3) the exercising of church discipline.

Our church's doctrine is pure and the ordinances are administered. But does the church of the twentieth century exercise corrective discipline? Christians today are concerned about discipleship. But are they committed enough to the principles of discipleship to confront and correct an erring disciple?

The following conversation took place between a church deacon and his new pastor. It reflects a very prevalent attitude toward the matter of confronting sinning saints:

"Pastor, I know you are still unpacking and getting moved into your office, but there is something you should know about one of our church members. I must tell you this in confidence, for, you see, I'm not supposed to know.

"John Doe, one of our trustees, has been involved in an adulterous relationship for several years.[1] He provides airline tickets for the woman and arranges for her to meet him in various cities where he does business. John's wife knows about the mistress and has been devastated by the messy affair. Yet she's remained faithful to her marriage commitment and is seeking to win her husband back—"

"My word, Steve, this is awful! John is a trustee, you say? How do you think we should handle this situation? What do you think we should do?"

"I don't think there is anything we can do, Pastor. In the first place, no one is supposed to know about this situation. In the second place, we can't ignore the fact that John contributes a great deal of money to this church. There is also John's family to consider. I'm sure they would find it quite embarrassing to have this family matter brought into the open. We're not just dealing with a

---

[1]The illustrations throughout this book are based on actual situations. To protect the privacy of the individuals and churches involved, however, the names, circumstances and revealing details have been altered.

kid who is cutting up. John is a successful businessman and a respected member of the community. It will have to be dealt with someday, but for now, well, let's just wait and see. . . ."

A Church Seriously Ill

The above conversation reflects the moral blight which has infected hundreds of churches in America. A quick glance at the spiritual thermometer of the twentieth-century church indicates that it is seriously ill. Christ said, however, that the "gates of hell will not prevail against" the church (Matt. 16:18, KJV). Therefore, the illness of the church is not terminal, but it is, nonetheless, serious.

The church today is suffering from an infection which has been allowed to fester. As an untreated boil oozes germ-infested pus and contaminates the whole body, so the church has been contaminated by sin and moral compromise. As an infection weakens the body by destroying its defense mechanisms, so the church has been weakened by this ugly sore. The church has lost its power and effectiveness in serving as a vehicle for social, moral and spiritual change. This illness is due, at least in part, to a neglect of church discipline.

Church discipline. It sounds severe—and rather old-fashioned. You may be thinking, *Isn't that what Nathaniel Hawthorne's* Scarlet Letter *was about? I thought church discipline went out with child spankings in favor of a more understanding, affirmative approach toward problems and problem people?* People today hesitate to talk about matters as serious as church discipline. Evangelist Luis Palau has remarked that church discipline "is one of the least talked about subjects within the church."[2] Many are afraid to discuss it. Most believers would rather talk about victorious Christian living.

Our pleasure-seeking society encourages everyone to "do your own thing." There is little accountability these days. Those in authority are often disregarded or openly mocked. It is much like the time of the Judges when "everyone did what was right in his own eyes" (Judg. 21:25). The result for ancient Israel was social, moral and political chaos. We face these same problems in twentieth-century America.

Christian leaders today are asking themselves if something can be done about the increasing worldliness of the church. They

---

[2]Luis Palau, "Discipline in the Church," *Discipleship Journal* (Issue 16, 1983), p.18.

see situations which might require discipline, but these leaders are unsure as to how to discipline. Pastors are wondering what other churches in their denomination are doing in this difficult area. Some have studied the matter, but church leaders have not yet arrived at clear conclusions as to what the Scripture teaches about church discipline. Many others struggle with how to *apply* the principles of church discipline in their ministry.

The Scriptural Solution

There is a need to search out what the Bible says about disciplining sinning saints. This book considers the issue biblically and provides insights into this rather sensitive, but absolutely imperative pastoral responsibility. Having surveyed hundreds of pastors from over sixty denominations, I will discuss the experiences, both positive and negative, of those churches which are attempting to apply God's Word in this area. Questions to be considered in this study include:

1. What is church discipline?
2. Why is church discipline necessary? What are the consequences of neglecting this ministry?
3. When is church discipline in order? What sins or offenses require discipline?
4. What steps should be taken to discipline a church member? What attitudes are essential to carrying out church discipline effectively?
5. What does Paul mean when he writes of delivering one over "to Satan for the destruction of his flesh" (1 Cor. 5:5)? Who has authority to administer church discipline?
6. What is the purpose of church discipline? Is it designed to punish, correct, or restore? What results should it be expected to achieve?
7. What place does forgiveness have in church discipline? When should it be extended?
8. What happens if the sinning saint does not respond to the disciplinary measures?
9. What steps should be followed in disciplining a pastor, deacon or church leader?
10. What are the dangers of church discipline? How can a lawsuit be avoided?
11. What are other pastors and churches in America doing about church discipline? How can churches work together more effectively to carry out church discipline?

The basic message of this book is this: *Church discipline is God's loving plan for restoring sinning saints*. God's purpose in disciplining His children is not to destroy their lives and end their ministries, but rather to restore them to fellowship and usefulness in the body of Christ. Restoration, not ruination, is the preeminent objective of church discipline. The writer of Hebrews expresses it well: "Therefore, strengthen the hands that are weak . . . so that the limb which is lame may not be put out of joint, but rather be healed" (Heb. 12:12–13).

Discipline and Discipleship

R. C. Sproul states, "The church is called not only to a ministry of reconciliation, but a ministry of nurture to those within her gates. Part of that nurture includes church discipline. . . ."[3]

Congregational discipline is really an act of discipleship which functions as the corollary of evangelism. Evangelism ministers to those outside the church who are in bondage to sin. Congregational discipline ministers to those within the church who are in bondage to sin. Marlin Jeschke remarks:

> In discipline, as in the presentation of the good news to the non-Christian, a person is presented the opportunity of being liberated from the power of sin in all its forms by coming under the rule of Christ and walking in His way.[4]

Church discipline may be broadly defined as *the confrontive and corrective measures taken by an individual, church leaders, or the congregation regarding a matter of sin in the life of a believer.*

Unlike the *Scarlet Letter,* biblical church discipline is not designed to punish. The Anabaptist pastor, Menno Simons (1496–1561), noted for his advocacy of church discipline, said, "The ban is not given to destroy but to build up."[5] Administered in a concerned and loving manner, church discipline will help sinning saints face the reality that their sinful actions are inconsistent with their profession of Christian faith. Thus, church discipline is designed to awaken people to their sin and move them

[3]R.C. Sproul, *In Search of Dignity* (Ventura, Calif.: Regal Books, 1983), p. 182.
[4]Marlin Jeschke, *Discipling the Brother* (Scottdale, Pa.: Herald Press, 1972, 1979), pp. 181–82.
[5]Menno Simons, "On the Ban: Questions and Answers" in *Spiritual and Anabaptist Writers*, eds. G. H. Williams and A. M. Mergal (Philadelphia: The Westminster Press, 1957), p. 266.

to repentance. Is this kind of caring confrontation taking place in your church? Should it be?

Biblical Principles Applied

In their runaway bestseller, *The One Minute Manager,* Kenneth Blanchard and Spencer Johnson offer business executives three secrets to increasing their productivity, profits, and prosperity. The third of these secrets is the "one minute reprimand." The procedure is designed to discipline for failure without attacking the employee's self-esteem. The suggestions they offer include the following:

1. Reprimand people immediately.
2. Tell people what they did wrong—be specific.
3. Tell people how you feel about what they did wrong.
4. Shake hands and let them know that you are on their side.
5. Remind them how much you value them.
6. Reaffirm that you think well of them, but not of their performance in this situation.
7. Realize that when the reprimand is over, it's over.[6]

Do these guidelines sound familiar? If you have been reading your Bible, they should. It is amazing to me that while the church has long since abandoned the practice of reprimand, secular businessmen are buying the concept hook, line and sinker. For twelve months *The One Minute Manager* was on the *New York Times* bestseller list! And the principles upon which the "one minute reprimand" is based come right from Scripture.

When will Christians recognize that the Bible contains a gold mine full of nuggets on successful personal relationships? There is no need to fear a loving, caring confrontation. Even Wall Street has decided that it is one of the secrets to success and productivity.

Correction Accomplished

Church discipline often fails. Spicy gossip about an offender's sin travels through the church grapevine more quickly than the proverbial greased lightning. Soon the offender is too embarrassed to come to church services, and the fallen saint leaves the church and never returns. It happens this way in many churches.

---

[6]Kenneth Blanchard and Spencer Johnson, *The One Minute Manager* (New York: Berkley Books, 1983), p. 59.

But it doesn't have to. Here is an example of church discipline that succeeds.

A church member had become involved in an adulterous relationship. Upon discovery of this situation, he was confronted first by the pastor, and then by the elders. At both meetings the young man refused to acknowledge his sin. The church leaders then concluded they would have to remove his name from the church role. At a public meeting of the church members, this situation was discussed and the church family agreed that removing the man's name from membership was in order. The offender was then informed of the discipline that had taken place.

Several weeks passed. Then one Sunday the former member attended the evening worship service of the church that had disciplined him. At that meeting he publicly and tearfully acknowledged he had sinned against God and his good wife. He expressed an attitude of repentance and requested to be restored to membership. On the basis of his sincere repentance, wrought in his heart by the Holy Spirit, the church family eagerly welcomed him back into their fellowship.

The Challenge Ahead

Is it possible for this kind of restorative church discipline to take place in your church and in congregations around our country? I believe it is. Is it possible to discipline and yet avoid division and disunity? Yes, if biblical principles are followed. As judgment must begin at the house of the Lord (1 Pet. 4:17), so purging the dross from our nation must begin with the purifying of our nation's churches.

In Rev. 3:19 Jesus commands the church of Laodicea to "be zealous, therefore, and repent." His invitation stands open to the church of the twentieth century. As we embark on this study, join me in praying for the pastors, teachers and leaders of our churches. May they hear and heed Christ's call to purity in His church. My hope and prayer is that the church will meet Christ at His coming, "having no spot or wrinkle or any such thing; but that she should be holy and blameless" (Eph. 5:27).

1
THE CHURCH WITHOUT DISCIPLINE

Having been recently divorced, Charlie decided to relocate and start a new life. He chose a small town where his college roommate and long-time friend was serving as pastor of a growing congregation—Bethel Community Church. Charlie, being warm and outgoing, was well received by the church. Someone provided him a cottage rent free until he could find work. The pastor, of course, was especially pleased to have such a good friend with whom to fellowship. A gifted teacher and musician, Charlie was soon leading singing and teaching a Sunday school class.

Several months after Charlie had become actively involved at Bethel Community Church, it was discovered that he had become sexually involved with a young single woman in the church. Public knowledge of the illicit relationship brought pressure for a confession. The two confessed and "repented." When it became known the young lady was pregnant, she cleared Charlie's name, claiming another man was involved. Since the matter had been "dealt with," Charlie continued his ministry of leading songs and teaching Sunday school.

Several months after the discovery of Charlie's illicit involvement, he announced his engagement to another woman. Feeling jilted, the former girlfriend then announced the child she was carrying was actually Charlie's.

As the wedding date approached, the associate pastor urged that disciplinary action be taken. The planned marriage was not in keeping with scriptural instructions for a divorced person (cf. 1 Cor. 7:11) and was causing many to believe that Charlie had not truly repented from his previous illicit involvement. Predictably, the pastor was very reluctant to initiate discipline against his good friend. The deacons advised the church family to "love Charlie back to the Lord."

Things continued to simmer at Bethel Community Church. People were asking questions that the pastor couldn't answer. Some thought Charlie ought at least to pay child support to the pregnant lover. Others were convinced stronger measures should be taken. Finally the unwed mother left the church. Sensing a lack of direction and commitment, several families subsequently left to fellowship elsewhere. Charlie went ahead and remarried.

There was no split at Bethel Community Church. The pastor was not asked to resign. There was no public scandal. Yet, though once growing and prospering, the church saw a significant decline in attendance. The associate pastor left. A year after the incident, people were still asking questions and finding the issue being sidestepped.

Bethel Community is another church without discipline. It has lost its purity, its power, and its potential for progress. To gain a fuller appreciation of the problems of a church without discipline, let us consider the case studies of two New Testament churches which neglected discipline.

Case Study No. 1: Corinth

Corinth is considered one of the most strategically located cities in the ancient world. Situated on the isthmus which links the Peloponnesus to mainland Greece, Corinth could control the major land route through Achaia (southern Greece). Corinth was a prosperous commercial center, boasting two fine ports, and was also a center of worship for Aphrodite, the Greek goddess of love. Paul ministered in Corinth for a year and a half, establishing a church that was at once his pride and despair. For though faith flourished there, so did sin.

In 1 Corinthians, Paul rebuked the Corinthians for their lack of discipline with regard to a known case of immorality in the church. Paul wrote: "It is actually reported that there is immorality among you, and immorality of such a kind as does not exist even among the Gentiles, that someone has his father's wife" (5:1).

The word "immorality" (*porneia*) is a general term for sexual misconduct, and in this context refers to an incestuous relationship between a young man and his stepmother ("his father's wife").[1] The New Testament expression, "to have a woman," means to marry her (cf. Matt. 14:4; 22:28; 1 Cor. 7:2, 29),[2] so it appears that this was a case of incestuous marriage. The Old Testament strictly prohibited such marriages (Lev. 18:6–18; Deut. 22:30). Cases of incest were not actually unknown among Gentiles; however, they were not common and did not meet with public approval.

How did the church at Corinth respond to this unsavory situation in her midst? The believers at Corinth had a serious problem with pride (cf. 4:6, 7, 18, 19). They were proud of their leaders, their wisdom, and their freedom. They suffered under the delusion that the church at Corinth was superior to the rest of the churches of Macedonia and Achaia. So blinded were they by their pride that they could not recognize the ugly flaw which had developed in their midst. Paul does not mean in verse two that they were "puffed up" because of this immorality (as if it were a grand expression of Christian freedom) but in spite of it.[3] They thought themselves so spiritually mature that the matter was of little consequence. A sin which should have overwhelmed them with grief left them inflated with complacency.

They could not plead ignorance. Paul reminds them in verse nine, "I wrote you in my letter not to associate with immoral people." This letter, which had been written earlier than 1 Corinthians and has since disappeared, specifically addressed the issue of disciplining sinning saints. Paul clarifies the meaning of his previous instructions in verse 11: "But actually, I wrote to you not to associate with any so-called brother if he should be an immoral person, or covetous, or an idolater, or a reviler, or a drunkard, or a swindler—not even to eat with such a one." Because of the church's failure to deal with this issue, Paul had to assert his apostolic authority to carry out disciplinary action against the offender.

The Corinthian church neglected its responsibility to exercise church discipline, and consequently it suffered. As the rotten

---

[1]For a thorough study of *porneia* in connection with Jesus' teaching on divorce, see my *The Divorce Myth* (Minneapolis: Bethany House Publishers, 1981), pp. 66–77.

[2]W. Harold Mare, "First Corinthians," in *The Expositor's Bible Commentary*, vol. 10, ed. Frank E. Gaebelein (Grand Rapids: Zondervan Publishing Company, 1976), p. 217.

[3]A.T. Robertson and Alfred Plummer, *The First Epistle of St. Paul to the Corinthians*, 2nd ed. (Edinburgh: T. & T. Clark, 1914), p. 96.

apple which spoils the entire barrel of good apples, one sin at Corinth led to another. Insensitivity to one moral issue led to compromise on others. The Corinthians engaged in lawsuits, misused their liberty, profaned the Lord's Supper, neglected the primacy of love, failed to regulate the use of their gifts, and questioned the resurrection. Church discipline seems to have been a watershed issue at Corinth. Its neglect led the way to a host of spiritual failures.

Case Study No. 2: Thyatira

Thyatira was an important manufacturing center situated on the Lycus River about 75 miles northeast of Ephesus. Dye manufacturing and garment-making were major industries at Thyatira. Lydia, Paul's convert at Philippi, was from Thyatira. She apparently was a regional sales representative for Thyatira's famous products, for Luke calls her "a seller of purple fabrics" (Acts 16:14). Thyatira was especially noted for its trade guilds, which were better organized than those of any other ancient city. The guild meetings, however, featured acts of pagan worship and immorality. Thyatira therefore was a rugged testing ground for the Christian gospel of grace.

The gospel may have been brought to the city by Lydia (Acts 16:14), or perhaps by one of Paul's disciples during the two years he preached at Ephesus (Acts 19:10). The fine church which was established there is commended in Rev. 2:19: "I know your deeds, and your love and faith and service and perseverance, and that your deeds of late are greater than at first."

But like the church at Corinth, the church at Thyatira was infected by a complacent neglect of immorality in her midst. Such complacency was encouraged by a false teacher referred to as "Jezebel." This name appears to have been deliberately chosen to elicit memories of King Ahab's Jezebel who promoted Baal worship in the Northern Kingdom (1 Kings 16:31; 18:19). Baal worship in Canaan was not only idolatrous, but promoted ritual prostitution. The worshipers of Baal performed sex acts with sacred priestesses in Baal's temple in order to cause the lustful Baal to copulate with his goddesses and thus fertilize the earth. As the Old Testament Jezebel's Baal worship promoted immorality in Israel, so did this false prophetess at Thyatira.

There was enormous pressure to be involved in immorality at Thyatira. Because the economic life of the citizens was dominated by the trade guilds, in which pagan religious practices were a criteria for membership, to refuse participation meant social isolation and economic hardship. Arguing that "there is no such thing as an idol in the world" (1 Cor. 8:4), "Jezebel" was suggesting that "believers need not undergo the privation which would follow from unwillingness to go along with the simple requirements of the trade guild."[4] That the religious feasts led to sexual promiscuity did not seem to trouble "Jezebel" and those who followed her (2:20, 21).

There was no large problem at Thyatira—simply a growing church evidencing deeds of love and faith. Just a bit of false teaching which led to a wee bit of immorality, and then, knowledge of "the deep things of Satan" (Rev. 2:24). Mounce summarizes the possible rationale of Jezebel:

> On the basis that a believer's spirituality is unaffected by what he does with his body, Jezebel could argue that the Thyatiran Christians ought to take part in the pagan guild feasts (even if they were connected with the deep things of Satan) and thus prove how powerless is evil to alter the nature of grace.[5]

How deceptive are the ways of Satan! It is amazing how far the church at Thyatira departed from the "straight and narrow way" due to a neglect in the area of discipline. And because the church didn't mete out discipline, the Lord promised He would (Rev. 2:22, 23). Not only did He bring tribulation and death to those involved in the wickedness, but He snuffed out the candle of the church. No testimony at all is better than a testimony to spiritual darkness.

The Results of Neglecting Discipline

The church that neglects to lovingly confront and correct its members is not being kind, generous, or gracious. Such a church is really hindering the Lord's work and the advance of Christ's kingdom. The church without discipline is a church without purity, power, and progress. We shall now consider these characteristics (or lack of them) individually.

---

[4]Robert H. Mounce, *The Book of Revelation* NICNT (Grand Rapids: Wm. B. Eerdmans Publishing Co., 1977), p. 103.
[5]Ibid., p. 106.

Lack of purity

Christ's work was not merely to save the church; it was also to sanctify the church. Paul writes:

> Christ also loved the church and gave Himself up for her; that He might sanctify her, having cleansed her by the washing of water with the word, that He might present to Himself the church in all her glory, having no spot or wrinkle or any such thing; but that she should be holy and blameless.
>
> Eph. 5:25–27

In view of His nearing return for His own, Christ has a deep interest in the purity of the church. Paul's words in 1 Cor. 5:6 reflect this concern: "Do you not know that a little leaven leavens the whole lump of dough?" It is the "rotten apple syndrome" again. A little impurity in the church can breed profusely. Warham Walker says it well:

> A slight gangrenous infection, if its progress be not stayed, will speedily pass through the whole body, prostrating its energies, and turning its comeliness into corruption. In like manner, offences committed by church members, if tolerated, "will increase unto more ungodliness" (1 Cor. 5:6; Heb. 12:15; 2 Tim. 2:16, 17).[6]

In 1 Cor. 5:7–8 Paul draws upon an Old Testament analogy to reinforce the call for purity in the church. The Jewish feast of Passover, which typifies Christ's sacrificial work as the Lamb of God, was followed by the feast of Unleavened Bread (Lev. 23:4–8). Before the feast of Unleavened Bread all leaven and leavened bread was to be removed from an Israelite's house and burned. Thus Paul says, "Clean out the old leaven, that you may be a new lump, just as you are in fact unleavened. For Christ our Passover also has been sacrificed."

Since Christ has offered His ultimate sacrifice, fulfilling the Old Testament type, the church has entered into the period of "unleavened bread." Paul continues, "Let us therefore celebrate the feast, not with old leaven, nor with the leaven of malice and wickedness, but with the unleavened bread of sincerity and truth" (1 Cor. 5:8). A neglect of discipline results in an impure church; and while we cannot get Christians out of the world, we can and should strive to get the world out of the church. So, argues Paul,

---

[6]Warham Walker, *Harmony in the Church: Church Discipline* (Rochester, N.Y.: Backus Book Publishers, 1981), pp. 76–77.

"Remove the wicked man from among yourselves" (1 Cor. 5:13).

Lack of power

Like most motorists, you probably have had your share of car problems. A problem which can cause a good deal of frustration is a lack of power when accelerating. The car hesitates, chugs, and sometimes stalls. Often these symptoms are caused by a dirty carburetor which inhibits the flow of fuel to the engine. Impurity in the carburetion system results in a loss of engine power.

This principle which we have seen illustrated in the mechanical realm is also true in the spiritual realm. The classic biblical example of this truth is found in Joshua 7, which tells of Achan's sin and Israel's defeat at Ai. The Israelites had embarked on the conquest of the Promised Land and had just experienced a tremendous victory at Jericho. Anticipating another great victory, Joshua sent 3,000 men to capture the small fortress city of Ai, but instead of another overwhelming victory, the Israelite forces were routed! As the Israelites fled, the men of Ai killed 36 of the Israelite warriors. Israel was defeated, the nation was demoralized, and Joshua was dismayed (Josh. 7:4–9). Ai was such a small city. Why had the Lord's army suffered such a humiliating defeat?

As Joshua called out to the Lord, seeking the reason for Israel's defeat, God spoke and revealed the root of the problem.

> Israel has sinned, and they have also transgressed My covenant which I commanded them. And they have even taken some of the things under the ban and have both stolen and deceived. Moreover, they have also put them among their own things. Therefore the sons of Israel cannot stand before their enemies; they turn their backs before their enemies, for they have become accursed.
>
> Josh. 7:11–12a

The Lord commanded Joshua to gather the Israelites together and determine the guilty party. It was soon discovered that Achan had taken some of the articles of Jericho which were "under the ban" and thus devoted to the Lord (Josh. 6:16–19). There was sin in the Israelite camp. And that sin resulted in a loss of military power for the people of Israel. Paul Enns observes:

> By taking some of the devoted things, Achan brought de-

struction on himself and the threat of destruction on the nation Israel. God viewed the entire nation as responsible, imputing the crime of Achan to all the people. One man sinned; the whole nation suffered.[7]

"Now hold it," you say. "Didn't Achan commit the sin? Why did the whole nation suffer for the failure of one man?"

While the biblical text acknowledges that Achan was the culprit, God clearly indicts the *whole* nation for the sin: "But the sons of Israel acted unfaithfully. . . . Israel has sinned. . ." (Josh. 7:1, 11). The guilt of the nation is based upon the principle of corporate solidarity. From a theological and divine viewpoint, the acts of one person can be attributed to the whole family of which he is a part (cf. Rom. 5:12; Heb. 7:5). Woudstra's comments are instructive: "The individual functions with the larger context of the community of which he is a part. Achan robbed the whole nation of the purity and holiness which it ought to possess before God."[8]

Sin in the camp of Israel resulted in a loss of blessing for the *whole* nation. As the congregation of Israel could not be indifferent regarding the sin of one of its members, so the local church cannot afford to neglect the sinning saint.

Lack of progress

A lack of purity always results in a lack of progress. Of course, there are stopgap measures. For example, higher octane gasoline may, for a short time, minimize the symptoms caused by a dirty carburetor. But the only real way to restore the mechanism to optimum performance is by overhauling the carburetor—not just by spraying its surfaces with "Gumout," but by cleaning every component and removing and replacing every faulty part. So, too, a church may hire an associate pastor, conduct an evangelistic crusade, or show a spectacular film series as a last-ditch effort to put more octane into declining attendance or to spray off the grime of spiritual lethargy. The people may sincerely desire to get back on the road to recovery and church growth. But none of these efforts will accomplish their objective if sin remains in the camp.

[7]Paul P. Enns, *Joshua* (Grand Rapids: Zondervan Publishing House, 1981), p. 64.
[8]Marten H. Woudstra, *The Book of Joshua* NICOT (Grand Rapids: Wm. B. Eerdmans Publishing Co., 1981), p. 120.

Only when the sin of Achan was confronted and the camp was purged could Israel go out in the power of God and conquer Ai (Josh. 8:1–19). If your carburetor is dirty, clean it. Only then will your engine will be restored to its full power. If there is sin in your camp, confront it. Only then will the church be able to tap God's infinite power to accomplish its mission.

Francis Schaeffer observes that Joshua 7 teaches the principle of the judgment of the people of God:

> It runs like this: (1) When we sin, God knows (because he exists and is infinite). (2) When we sin, the blessing slows or stops. It can even stop for a whole group on the basis of the sin of one or a few. (3) There will be judgment either from ourselves in confessing our sin or from God. (4) If we return, the blessing rolls on again.[9]

The church that seeks God's blessing cannot afford to neglect the purity of its body. Joshua 7 illustrates how the disobedience of one person can bring defeat to the whole congregation. The church that fails to lovingly confront and correct such a sinning saint will not just suffer a lack of purity. It will experience a loss of spiritual power and victory. There will be no victory at Ai while there is sin in Achan's tent.

The Michael Esses Story

What happens when Christians either neglect or tolerate on-going sin in the life of a professing believer? Betty Esses DeBlase, the former wife of the popular author and speaker, Michael Esses, gives chilling testimony on how easily believers can gloss over sin. In her book, *Survivor of a Tarnished Ministry*, Betty Esses tells about a dark side of her husband that most people never knew.[10]

While Michael Esses had an impeccable public image, his former wife asserts that he lied about his rabbinical ordination, was unfaithful throughout twenty-eight years of marriage, and dealt himself hundreds of thousands of dollars "under the table." According to Mrs. DeBlase, his bestselling autobiography, *Michael, Michael, Why Do You Hate Me?*, was largely his own fabrication.

The startling fact is that many of Michael Esses' associates,

---

[9]Francis A. Schaeffer, *Joshua and the Flow of Biblical History* (Downers Grove: InterVarsity Press, 1975), p. 117.

[10]Betty Esses DeBlase, *Survivor of a Tarnished Ministry: The True Story of Michael and Betty Esses* (Orange, Calif.: Truth Publishers, Inc., 1983).

including his wife, knew of his dishonesty and unfitness for ministry. So why did they gloss over these matters? Maybe because they liked his style, his drawing power. Or maybe they feared what others would think if Esses were exposed.

Tragically, this story illustrates a pattern seen in hundreds of other cases. The lives of many Christians are not significantly different from Michael Esses'. But the greatest tragedy in the church today is that many people know of these situations but fail to do anything about them. The principle of mutual accountability needs rediscovery in many of our churches and fellowships across the country.

While the sinner is clearly accountable for his own actions, the Bible implies that those who observe a sin and fail to warn the guilty of its consequences shall be held in account (Prov. 24:11, 12). As a watchman in Israel, Ezekiel was to warn the people of the penalties of their disobedience. The wicked were accountable for their response to the prophet, but Ezekiel knew he was accountable before God to issue the warning: "When I say to the wicked, 'You shall surely die'; and you do not warn him or speak out to warn the wicked from his wicked way that he may live, that wicked man shall die in his iniquity, but his blood I will require at your hand" (Ezek. 3:18).

Christians must rise up together and take a bold stand against ungodly behavior and impurity in the church. Only by confronting and correcting our sinning saints will the purified church enjoy the divine power and spiritual dynamic for a successful and lasting ministry.

2
THE PATTERN FOR CHURCH DISCIPLINE

I've been disciplined. During my childhood and youth I was regularly and consistently disciplined by my loving parents who wanted me to become an obedient and God-honoring young man. That discipline took various forms during different periods of my life. As a child, I was required to "fetch a switch" when I displayed an attitude of rebellion against my parents' authority. I don't believe I'll ever forget the lickin' I received the first (and last) time I stuck out my tongue at my father! "I was just licking my lips," I vainly argued as he went for the paddle.

Later in my adolescent years, my parents discontinued the physical discipline, but called me to accountability by threatening the loss of certain privileges. Failure to be home from a date by 11:30 p.m. meant no use of the car the next weekend. Leaving my girlfriend's house at 11:25, I set speed records for crosstown travel in my attempts to be home by the 11:30 deadline!

As my parents have disciplined me, so has my heavenly Father. Well do I remember one night when I woke up with a severe pain in my lower abdomen. As I lay in bed, the pain increased. Finally, I rose and began walking around in an attempt to relieve the discomfort. Was it something I had eaten? Was I having an attack of appendicitis? Was this the beginning of a stroke?

On the verge of panic, I asked the Lord to take care of me and to restore me to well-being. As I was praying, I realized there was an area of my life in which things were not right. It wasn't a major issue from the world's perspective. It was one of those things that Christians might dismiss as "culturally relative." Nevertheless, it seemed God was bringing this issue to my attention through my pain. I confessed it as sin, asked forgiveness, and appropriated the cleansing of the cross (1 John 1:9). As I concluded my prayer, the pain began to ease. Within ten seconds it was completely gone. I have never experienced that pain again. Coincidence? Some would argue that it was, but I believe that attack was by divine design. I had been disciplined.

We must recognize that not all physical affliction is the result of sin. This is proven by the experience of Job who was afflicted by Satan (Job 1:1, 22), by the illness of Lazarus whom Jesus raised from the dead (John 11:4), and by the predicament of the man who was born blind, not because of some sin his parents had committed, but "that the works of God might be displayed in him" (John 9:3). Although God does use physical illness for purposes other than discipline, He apparently used my discomfort to draw my attention to an area in which I was missing His mark. Having accomplished its purpose, the affliction was removed.

The subject addressed in this book, however, is *church* discipline. But before focusing on the discipline which the church is authorized to carry out, we must give attention to the pattern of discipline which God exemplifies in dealing with His children. Heb. 12:5–13 presents the divine pattern of discipline which the church of Christ must model. Here we see that discipline is the "trump card" of God's grace, designed to move us to repentance and restore us to fellowship with himself.

In Hebrews 12, Christians are challenged to "lay aside every encumbrance," and "run with endurance the race that is set before us" (12:1). Christ is presented as an example to those who want to learn how to run this race (12:2). His endurance through suffering is set forth as an incentive and encouragement for believers experiencing trial. The key idea here is that Christ *endured* through difficult times. Endurance is one of the most crucial Christian virtues in times of waiting and trial (Gal. 6:9). The writer of Hebrews expects that by considering Christ's example, his readers will "not grow weary and lose heart" (12:3).

The author proceeds in verses 4–13 to consider the blessings and benefits of divine discipline. God's discipline is designed to correct and restore a sinning saint. This discipline and its objective provides an excellent model for discipline within our churches.

The Loving Motive—Heb. 12:4–6

The writer of Hebrews points out in verses 4–6 that God's discipline of His children is motivated by love, rather than by anger or wrath. He declares in verse 4 that although the Hebrew Christian readers of his epistle had suffered much (10:32), none of them had yet been martyred ("resisted to the point of shedding blood") as had Stephen (Acts 7) and James (Acts 12).

Then he reminds the readers of the truth Solomon expressed so well in Prov. 3:11–12: "My son, do not regard lightly the discipline of the Lord, nor faint when you are reproved by Him; for those whom the Lord loves He disciplines, and He scourges every son whom He receives."

The link between "love" and "discipline" is also acknowledged by Christ in His words to the church at Laodicea: "Those whom I love, I reprove and discipline; be zealous therefore, and repent" (Rev. 3:19). The world often views discipline as the expression of anger and hostility, but according to God's Word, proper discipline is the expression and outworking of love.

The knowledge that God disciplines those He loves serves as a deterrent from sin for believers. This principle applies as well in the area of child discipline. At the Laneys' we keep our "helping stick" in a prominent place in our kitchen. It serves as a faithful reminder to our three young children that crime doesn't pay. I wonder how many times my children have run through the kitchen in the pursuit of some dastardly deed, spotted the paddle and repented before carrying out the offense!

The word used for discipline, *paideia* (Heb. 12:6), speaks of the upbringing, education and training of a child. In Eph. 6:4, Paul recognizes two major types of discipline which parents are given authority to administer: (1) training by act ("discipline") and (2) training by word ("instruction"). The discipline which parents use most frequently is corrective—a response to a child's display of rebellion or disobedience. This may take the form of a spanking or the loss of privileges. Preventive discipline is also an important aspect of child training. This involves spending time with the child, listening to him, and creating an atmosphere in which he may respond positively to correction.

The second type of discipline is that of training by word— instruction, encouragement or reproof. Eli's great failure was in this area. When his sons sinned and dishonored God, "he did not rebuke them" (1 Sam. 3:13). But both types of discipline— training by act and training by word—must be applied by parents desiring to rear their children successfully. After all, both are applied by our loving heavenly Father in His dealings with straying saints.

There are two improper ways to respond to parental discipline: to despise it or to despair of it. Some children shrug off discipline as another evidence of the "generation gap." Other children become overwhelmed by their inability to meet their parents' standards and expectations. These two responses are grounded in the child's failure to recognize and appreciate that parental discipline is motivated by love.

Similarly, those whom God disciplines must beware of despising God's chastening. Neither should they despair of it. As painful as the process is, such chastening represents the gracious dealings of an infinitely loving God! Those whom He loves, He disciplines. Those whom He receives, He "scourges." The reference to scourging, the act of flogging with a whip, implies that discipline may be physically painful. Nonetheless, it is always motivated by love.

As a parent, I find physical discipline an unpleasant task I would rather avoid. I don't like the spankings, the screams or the tears. I desperately wish there was an easier way to carry out my parental responsibility in childrearing. But I cannot escape the fact that Scripture authorizes parents to "use the rod." And in some circumstances, it is the best way to deal with the disobedience and rebellion of young children.

Only one thing moves me to spank my child: love. I'm not interested in spanking the neighbor's kid or anyone else's children—not that they don't sometimes need it! But my overwhelming love for my own children demands that I allow no inappropriate behavior to go unchecked. My love forces me to act so that my children will someday be well trained young people whose lives truly honor the Lord. God's love works the same way, only infinitely more so.

The Family Relationship—Heb. 12:7–9

The writer of Hebrews points out in verses 7–9 that God's discipline occurs in a family relationship. When believers experience divine discipline, their heavenly Father is dealing with them as "sons." The writer drives the point home in verse 7 with the rhetorical question, "For what son is there whom his father does not discipline?" The implied answer is "none!" All faithful and committed fathers will, on occasion, have to exercise loving discipline. All sons endure discipline. Even God's Son "learned obedience from the things which He suffered" (Heb. 5:8).

The writer notes also, in verse 8, that discipline signifies a vital relationship with one's father: "But if you are without discipline, of which all have become partakers, then you are illegitimate children and not sons." The term "illegitimate" is used to describe those who are without discipline. In the Roman world, an illegitimate child did not share the rights of inheritance along with other progeny. An illegitimate child was denied the privileges and benefits of the father-son relationship. The benefits included an inheritance *and* discipline.

In the same manner, one of the benefits of spiritual sonship is discipline. Divine discipline in the life of a believer, according to F. F. Bruce, stands "as a token that he is really a beloved son."[1] The absence of discipline in the life of a backslidden Christian reflects the absence of a bona-fide "father-child" relationship with God.

Verse 8 emphasizes the sobering thought that a Christian who is involved in sin will most assuredly be disciplined by God. If that discipline does not occur, however, there is reason to question the validity of that person's profession of faith. Perhaps the individual has been involved in "churchianity" instead of true, biblical Christianity. The lack of divine discipline in the life of a church member who persists in sinning may indicate that the person is in fact unsaved—not a genuine member of God's family (cf. Matt. 7:15–23; Titus 1:16; 1 John 3:6–10).

The proper response to discipline is revealed in verse 9. "Furthermore, we had earthly fathers to discipline us, and we respected them; shall we not much rather be subject to the Father of spirits, and live?" The expression, "Father of spirits," simply refers to our spiritual Father (God) in contrast to our human fathers.[2] The writer argues that respect for one's earthly parents has some spiritual implications: If we respect and submit to the authority of our parents as they exercise discipline, there is even greater reason to respect and submit to God's discipline. While earthly fathers sometimes make mistakes as they attempt to carry out discipline, our heavenly Father's discipline is always correctly and justly applied. Those who are true sons are partakers of God's perfect discipline. This discipline is a clear evidence of their new birth and spiritual life.

---

[1]F.F. Bruce, *The Epistle to the Hebrews*, NICNT (Grand Rapids: Wm. B. Eerdmans Publishing Co., 1964), p. 357.

[2]Homer A. Kent, Jr., *The Epistle to the Hebrews* (Grand Rapids: Baker Book House, 1972), p. 263.

The Wholesome Benefits—Heb. 12:10–13

Divine discipline, wrought in God's infinite love, yields wholesome benefits. In verse 10 the writer of Hebrews compares the discipline of human fathers with that of our heavenly Father. They disciplined us according to what "seemed best to them." Our heavenly Father, on the other hand, disciplines us "for our good." The writer is contrasting "the brief authority of parents, and their liability to error . . . with the pure love and eternal justice of God."[3] While human fathers sometimes make mistakes and thus harm their children, God's purposes and methods in discipline are always to our benefit. Such discipline is intended to move believers along the path of Christian living toward sanctification "that we may share in His holiness" (cf. 1 Pet. 1:15, 16).

The writer acknowledges in verse 11 that all discipline, whether by human fathers or by our heavenly Father, causes sorrow rather than joy. Evangelist Billy Graham would undoubtedly concur. "The rod is considered old-fashioned in many homes," he says. "Psychiatrists say it will warp your personality. When I did something wrong as a boy, my mother warped part of me, but it wasn't my personality."[4]

Painful as it is, however, discipline yields rewards: "Yet to those who have been trained by it, afterwards it yields the peaceful fruit of righteousness." (Billy Graham's life certainly is clear evidence of the rewards of loving parental discipline.) But these rewards are not immediately realized. The athlete, for example, knows that only after the training period is completed will he fully appreciate the benefits of his regular, rigorous workouts.

The ultimate rewards do not always seem so obvious. We see the principle illustrated in this story: A small boy was floating his model boat on the pond in a city park when suddenly a light breeze forced the craft out of the child's reach. The boy's desperate attempts to retrieve it caught the attention of an elderly gentleman who then came to assist. But the child was horrified when the man started tossing rocks in the direction of the boat! Then the boy realized the rocks were going over the boat and making ripples which pushed the boat back to shore.

So it is with God's discipline. When we stray from Him, it

---

[3]F. W. Farrar, *The Epistle of Paul the Apostle to the Hebrews* (Cambridge: At the University Press, 1896), p. 177.

[4]Bill Adler, ed. *The Wit and Wisdom of Billy Graham* (New York: Random House, 1967), n.p.

may appear He is throwing rocks at us. But really He is using the violent ripples to bring us back to Himself.

Verses 12 and 13 contain two admonitions which apply the truths of verses 5–11. The key to benefiting from God's discipline is proper response. The Hebrew Christians had been responding improperly; they had allowed themselves to become disheartened and discouraged by their trials. They were thus in danger of becoming spiritually paralyzed—permanently disabled in their Christian lives, having failed to appropriate the benefits of God's discipline. Drawing on two Old Testament texts, the writer challenges them to "strengthen the hands that are weak and the knees that are feeble, and make straight paths for your feet" (12:12–13a; cf. Isa. 35:3; Prov. 4:26). In other words, "Shake off your paralyzing discouragement and straighten yourselves up again to full strength." This strengthening and straightening must be achieved by the power of the Holy Spirit (Rom. 8:3–4) as believers "fix their eyes on Jesus, the author and perfecter of faith" (Heb. 12:2).

The last line of verse 13 reveals God's purpose in the disciplinary process. He intends that the "limb which is lame" not be "put out of joint, but rather be healed." God's design in discipline, therefore, is not to disable permanently those who have experienced the crippling effects of sin. Rather, His purpose is to *heal* and *restore* the repentant to spiritual usefulness.

A Biblical Example

There are many examples in the Old Testament of God's discipline in the lives of His people. God disciplined Moses (Deut. 32:48–52), Miriam (Num. 12:1–15), Saul (1 Sam. 16:14), and king Manasseh (2 Chron. 33:1–20). One of the classic examples of God's discipline in the Old Testament is His dealings with David after his adultery with Bathsheba and his murder of Uriah.

Second Samuel 11 certainly marks the low point of David's career. Instead of being out in the field with his army, David was hanging around Jerusalem with time on his hands. A sleepless night and a glimpse of a beautiful woman served as the catalysts for David's undisciplined desires, and soon he was having an adulterous affair with the wife of one of his soldiers. When Bathsheba reported she was pregnant, David sought to "cover his tracks" by calling her husband home from the battlefield for a night with his wife. Uriah refused such pleasures while his fellow soldiers were in the field, so David resorted to further treachery. He plotted Uriah's death.

At David's request, Joab commanded a field maneuver which left Uriah isolated and unprotected, so although Uriah was killed in battle, his death was the result of David's murderous plot. After Bathsheba's time of mourning was over, David sent for her and she became his wife. The biblical account ends with this brief divine commentary: "But the thing that David had done was evil in the sight of the LORD" (2 Sam. 11:27).

I am continually amazed at the deceitfulness of sin, which has been demonstrated over and over again in the lives of Christians who succumb to sin and then deny its existence in their lives. God must deal with sin-blinded saints drastically. He had to use Nathan, the king's prophet and counselor, to make David face the issue of his own sinfulness (2 Sam. 12:1–12). When confronted with the reality of his gross misconduct, David confessed and said to Nathan, "I have sinned against the LORD" (2 Sam. 12:13).

David was a man after God's own heart (1 Sam. 13:14; Acts 13:22), so although he had sinned greatly, his heart remained spiritually sensitive. On the basis of David's confession (cf. Ps. 51), Nathan assured David that he was forgiven and that he would not die for his crime (cf. Lev. 20:10). Then Nathan declared, "However, because by this deed you have given occasion to the enemies of the LORD to blaspheme, the child also that is born to you shall surely die" (2 Sam. 12:14). The Lord struck the child with a severe illness. Seven days later the child died.

Out of infinite love and boundless grace, God disciplined David for his adultery with Bathsheba. The death of a child is maybe the most grievous experience a parent can endure, yet God brought such severe discipline to David's life in order to chasten and correct him.

This discipline was also designed to vindicate God's reputation. The sin of David had given the enemies of God occasion to speak against Him because of the moral failure of His choice servant—"What kind of God is Yahweh whose anointed king takes the wife of his own soldier?" Public sin has public consequences. David had to be disciplined by God in such a manner as to show all Israel, and its neighbors, His strong disapproval, and thus quiet such slanderous talk.

Other examples of God's discipline could be examined, but this one is sufficient to show that His discipline is designed to restore sinning saints. God didn't kill David, although he deserved death. Seeing the brokenness of David's heart, God accepted his sincere confession of sin and moved him along the path of discipline to restore the king to spiritual usefulness. As in David's case, God's discipline is sometimes severe. But it is always wrought in love and designed to produce the fruit of holiness and righteousness in the lives of God's children.

Biblical church discipline involves lovingly confronting the believer (leader or layman) who has strayed into sin. It may require calling on witnesses to challenge those who refuse to acknowledge their sin. It may necessitate a public rebuke and removal from membership in the case of those who persist in wrongdoing.

Church discipline is not designed to punish but to restore. It is an act of healing. Yes, it may be painful; as in the application of iodine, pain is the price of a cleansed wound. It prepares the way for restoration. Through the pain of confrontation, rebuke, confession and forgiveness, the sinner is brought back into fellowship with Christ and His church. Such restoration is church discipline's ultimate goal.

3
A TIME FOR DISCIPLINE

When Sam graduated from seminary, he was called to pastor a church in the Midwest. Not long into his ministry he found himself involved in a very difficult counseling situation which required spending two days in court with a church member who had committed a crime. The trial was receiving much coverage by the press. The man had repented to the Lord, but realized, because of the public exposure he was receiving, that if he did not express his repentance before the congregation, he would never be able to face his friends again. He was becoming increasingly miserable as he imagined what others might be thinking about him.

Finally, the moment came. During a regular service Sam read Galatians 6 and other passages on forgiveness while his wife took all children to another room. The offender came forward and confessed his sin, asking the congregation's forgiveness and acceptance. Sam then asked for all who forgave the man to come forward. The entire church body responded and lined up to shake his hand or hug him and his wife. This was true restoration.

In Ecclesiastes, Solomon declares, "There is an appointed time for everything. And there is an appointed time for every event under heaven" (3:1). There is a time for tears and a time for laughter; a time to tear down and a time to build up; a time to be silent and a time to speak. Is there a time for discipline? When is church discipline appropriate, and for what sins should it be administered?

Difficulties with Initiating Church Discipline

Church discipline, applied strictly according to biblical guidelines, is a rare occurrence these days. During earlier times church discipline was a regular part of church life. In Scotland, for instance, during the time of John Knox, church elders were expected to visit the homes of the parishioners and inquire whether there had been any quarrels; and any family members who had were to be reconciled before they received communion. Only those who had received metal tokens of fitness would be allowed to participate in the Lord's Table.[1] In many churches, counseling has now replaced discipline. Much of what, in an earlier era, demanded action such as excommunication now calls for an "I'm OK, you're OK" session. One pastor writes of this, "I think we sometimes think in terms of long-term counseling to solve problems rather than discipline." People have come to associate church discipline with heresy hunts, witch burnings, intolerance and oppression. Church discipline, to most people, does not seem consistent with our individualistic society.

In studying this subject, Maryland pastor Mark Littleton surveyed several prominent pastors and church leaders. He discovered five main hindrances to the effective use of church discipline: (1) People wonder whether discipline will do any good; (2) people are unclear as to which sins we are to discipline; (3) people fear the outcome; (4) people associate discipline with excommunication, church courts, and intolerance; and (5) people have few models of positive discipline to imitate and do not know how to "speak the truth in love," or "admonish the unruly," or "restore those caught in a fault."[2]

I discovered similar obstacles. Fifty percent of the pastors I surveyed acknowledged there had been situations in their ministries where discipline was needed, but no action was taken. They cited three major hindrances to administration of church discipline: (1) Fear of the consequences or outcome, (2) ignorance of the proper procedures, and (3) preference for avoiding problems. Let us consider these and other hindrances individually.

Fear of the outcome

Many of the pastors surveyed cited "fear of rejection," "fear of reprisal," or "fear of a church split" as a reason why they

---

[1]Gene P. Heideman, "Discipline and Identity," *Reformed Review,* 35 (Fall 1981), p. 18.
[2]Mark R. Littleton, "Church Discipline: A Remedy for What Ails the Body," *Christianity Today* (May 8, 1981), pp. 30–31.

sometimes took no disciplinary action. A Baptist pastor writes, "The deacons are afraid to discipline the erring man. He was a very powerful figure, had been in the church for twenty years, and was a leader in the community."

Much of this fear has resulted from harsh and improper discipline. Paige Patterson, Director of the Criswell Center at the First Baptist Church in Dallas, explains, "The over-reaction of most Southern Baptist congregations to the abuses in church discipline in the remote past have made them very slow to return to the scriptural practice."

Fear for the outcome of church discipline is a real issue for those who shepherd God's flock. Every pastor must wrestle with the fear of personal confrontation, of giving offense, of being misunderstood or rejected, of driving away church members. These fears can't be denied, but God has the answer for them. In 1 John 4:18 the Apostle declares, "There is no fear in love, but perfect love casts out fear. . . ." Discipline carried out in anger, malice, revenge, or a desire to punish will generate hostility and give a pastor reason to fear. Loving, caring, sensitive confrontation, however, is the only kind of discipline that can ever succeed. God's love can conquer our fears and give Christian leaders the courage necessary for caring confrontation (cf. Ps. 34:4).

Ignorance of the procedures

Limited understanding of the biblical teaching on church discipline has handicapped many Christian leaders in fulfilling this responsibility. Many pastors who have faced a problem needing discipline, but took no action, blame their own ignorance or that of the congregation. One pastor from a large denomination recalls, "No one knew who should do it." A pastor from a fundamentalist church says he failed to take action because of his "uncertainty as to what action should be taken." Another pastor mentions a "lack of consensus among the congregation as to what ought to be done." Some pastors explain that the situations in which they failed to act occurred when they were young ministers. Their knowledge of disciplinary procedures and willingness to confront difficult situations increased as they matured in the ministry.

Perhaps our Bible schools and seminaries have been at fault for not providing in-depth teaching on the biblical procedures for church discipline. I recently examined the catalogs of eight major seminaries and found only one which mentions church discipline in any of the course descriptions. Granted, the subject may be discussed in some courses, but it appears church discipline has not received major emphasis as an integral aspect of seminary curriculum. Perhaps this will change as the subject continues to receive much attention from the media, both religious and secular. It would seem appropriate that seminary students be required to study this difficult issue.

Preference for avoiding problems

Except for those who might suffer from a martyr complex, most Christian leaders, myself included, prefer to avoid problems. We are not seeking trouble. The difficulties which might require church discipline are frequently not in accord with the major objective we are pursuing for the church. These problems sidetrack us, consuming our energy and time. As one pastor put it, "We don't want to rock the boat." Often busy pastors avoid the problem with the expectation that it will eventually go away or that the culprits will leave the church.

Problems can be ignored, but they can't be avoided. If we ignore them, they will be assimilated into the history and character of the church. Certain issues may become "dormant," but will later spring to life to haunt both the church family and church leaders. An associate pastor mentioned a time when three different young women had become pregnant out of wedlock, yet no action was taken. Leaders avoided confrontation—and as a result the problem of immorality remains. It will continue to afflict that church body until it is dealt with scripturally. Such confrontation, of course, takes spiritual courage on the part of the church and its leaders. But failure to do so is virtually equivalent to writing the church's obituary.

Will it do any good?

In many cases where some sort of disciplinary action is executed, the person or persons at fault simply leave the church. Haddon Robinson, president of Denver Seminary, refers to this as the "consumer mentality." He says, "If they like the product, they stay. If they do not, they leave. They can no more imagine a church disciplining them than they could a store that sells goods disciplining them."

Candidates for church membership need to be carefully instructed that joining a church is quite different from joining a country club. When people join a church they become members of a spiritual family. They must commit themselves to diligently participate in the church's ministries and to support the rest of the Body. Church discipline will accomplish its objective only when Christians are committed to one another and to those giving leadership in this area.

What sins are worthy of discipline?

There have been extremes on both sides of this issue. One pastor reports that a good number of his parishioners joined his church after being excommunicated by their own denomination for attending a Baptist church's worship service! On the other hand, there is the case of the pastor who divorced his wife, married his secretary, and stayed on as pastor with his church's blessing. Both extremes are unbiblical. The Bible does provide clear direction on this matter, and the specific texts will be considered shortly.

Unbiblical attitudes regarding church discipline

To some people, church discipline smacks of the medieval Inquisition—a reign of terror, of religious extremism. Christians therefore face the challenge of demonstrating, both to the church and the world, that corrective discipline is a family matter motivated and directed by love. The body of Christ is a spiritual family, whose members enter by new birth.

Membership in a family implies responsibility and accountability. I think of the many times I have checked up on my brothers and sisters to take a pulse on their spiritual health or their marital life, or help direct them in career decisions. Because they are members of my family, I would literally travel to any point on the globe to help a brother or sister in need. Don Bubna, senior pastor of Salem Alliance Church, writes concerning this, "As a church family we are equally responsible and accountable to one another. Effective discipline takes place in the context of these relationships."[3] Only by seeing this kind of example will

---

[3]Donald L. Bubna, "Redemptive Love: The Key to Church Discipline," *Leadership Journal* 2 (Summer 1981), p. 78.

"fringe" Christians and the world develop a more positive attitude toward this essential element of church life and practice.

Scarcity of positive models

Lack of precedent and positive models inhibits the exercise of church discipline. Many churches are simply not used to disciplining their members. When discipline does occur, it is frequently too timid, which simply encourages the continuance of the problem. Or it is too brash and abrasive and encourages others to become drill sergeants or executioners. Church leaders must model the kind of firm, but *loving* and *caring*, confrontation that should be taking place in their congregations.

The difficulties with initiating church discipline can seem awesome. But they are not insurmountable. From man's perspective, changing the attitudes of many church members about discipline seems impossible. But with God all things are possible (Matt. 19:26). God delights in taking on situations which to men appear impossible. He then effects victories which testify to the greatness of His redemptive love.

Discipline in the History of the Church

While the church in the twentieth century seems to have placed a low priority on the matter of corrective discipline, this has not been the case historically. Since the time of the early church, discipline has been recognized as an essential practice and distinctive of true, biblical Christianity. (A well-documented summary of the church's thinking on this subject is provided by Marlin Jeschke in his book *Discipling the Brother*.[4])

The New Testament contains abundant evidence of the practice of discipline by the apostolic church (Matt. 18:15–20; Acts 5:1–11; 1 Cor. 5:1–5; 2 Cor. 2:5–11; Gal. 2:11–14; 6:1; 2 Thess. 3:6–15). That church discipline was a prominent concern of the church in the post-apostolic period—through the first two or three centuries—is made clear by the debate over the possibility of forgiveness for sins committed after conversion. As persecution against Christians increased, there was also the question of how to deal with those who denied the faith under persecution, but were afterward genuinely repentant. Could they be rein-

---

[4]Marlin Jeschke, *Discipling the Brother* (Scottdale, Pa.: Herald Press, 1972), pp. 21–40.

stated in the church, and under what conditions?

These questions and issues led to the development of a recognized method of penance. According to the *Apostolic Constitutions,* a treatise of A.D. 252–270 from Syria, the offender was to be brought before the church, examined whether he be truly penitent, and then directed to continue in a state of mortification for two to seven weeks, depending upon the nature of the offense. Only then could he be absolved and readmitted to full fellowship. A person under such discipline engaged in "dramatic acts of remorse is evidence of genuine repentance—sackcloth and ashes, weeping at the door of the church, and interceding with the elders for readmission."[5]

By the fourth century the church had developed a rigorous system outlining the steps to restoration and the duration of penance. During this period, sin was taken very seriously and discipline—though restricted primarily to murder, unchastity, and idolatry—was very severe.

In the Middle Ages, due to the influence of the monastic orders, there developed the viewpoint that penance could be a private matter between the offender and the parish priest. The church no longer required public confession and penance. It no longer required the offender to appear in public for absolution. This would be handled in private by the priest. Public censure and penance continued, however, for the more notorious and scandalous offenses. With the Fourth Lateran Council in 1215, mandatory annual confession became required to maintain one's standing in the church. Failure to appear before the priest at least once a year would lead to excommunication and denial of Christian burial.

Although Martin Luther led the Reformation by throwing off such excesses as indulgences for sins one is likely to commit, he was hesitant in dealing with the subject of church discipline. His *Kirchenordnung* ("Church Order") contains no directions for penance, confession, or banning unrepentant sinners from communion. But Luther did practice church discipline and called upon others to do so. He held that most confrontation and correction should come from the preaching of the Word, but that exclusion from communion could serve as a last resort. On several occasions he advocated that those who failed to respond to

---

[5]Ibid., p. 22.

the ban from the Lord's Supper be given over to secular authorities and exiled.

The Swiss Reformer, Ulrich Zwingli, was more aggressive in the ordering of church discipline. With his strong sense of the oneness of church and state, he held that Christian magistrates ought to function as elders within the church in the administration of discipline. The magistrates possessed the right of excommunication.

Of the major Reformers, John Calvin made the greatest contribution toward the ordering of church discipline. In his *Institutes,* he writes:

> As the saving doctrine of Christ is the soul of the Church, so discipline forms the ligaments which connect the members together, and keep each in its proper place. Whoever, therefore, either desire the abolition of all discipline, or obstruct its restoration, whether they act from design or inadvertency, they certainly promote the entire dissolution of the Church.[6]

So important was church discipline to Calvin that he made the acceptance of his views a condition for his return to Geneva in 1541. He insisted on the church's independence of civil authorities, but looked to the magistrates to provide support for the church's decisions and enforcement of its decreed penalities.

The *Belgic Confession* (1561), which grew out of the Reformation, identifies church discipline as one of the marks of the true church:

> The marks by which the true Church is known are these: if the pure doctrine of the gospel is preached therein; if she maintains the pure administration of the sacraments as instituted by Christ; if church discipline is exercised in punishing of sin; in short, if all things are managed according to the pure Word of God, all things contrary thereto rejected, and Jesus Christ acknowledged as the only Head of the Church.

The Heidelberg Catechism, introduced into the churches and schools of Heidelberg, Germany in 1563, also contains a strong statement on the important place of discipline in the church.

The great *Westminster Confession of Faith,* completed in 1646, devotes a full chapter to "Church Censures." These are affirmed as:

---

[6]John Calvin, *Institutes of the Christian Religion*, 2 vols., ed. John T. McNeill (Philadelphia: The Westminster Press, 1960), p. 1,238 (Book IV, Chapter XII, Section 10).

. . . necessary for the reclaiming and gaining of offending brethren, for deterring of others from the like offences, for purging out of that leaven which might infect the whole lump, for vindicating the honour of Christ, and the holy profession of the gospel, and for preventing the wrath of God, which might justly fall upon the church, if they should suffer His covenant, and the seals thereof, to be profaned by notorious and obstinate offenders.

It also lists admonition, suspension from participation in the Lord's Supper for a season, and excommunication from the church as appropriate measures by which discipline may be administered.

Church discipline was an important part of the Anabaptist movement, as shown by the *Schleitheim Confession* of 1527. Menno Simons, an Anabaptist and founder of the Mennonites, wrote three tracts on the subject. His views were not as extreme as some have accused. He was a firm advocate of discipline, but emphasized that its purpose was to edify, not destroy.

In the seventeenth century, Scottish Presbyterians applied discipline rigorously and sought state support to carry out disciplinary measures. The Puritans in England also held to rigorous discipline, but developed a doctrine of church discipline which was applied independent of secular authorities. John Wesley, founder of Methodism, was a strong advocate of discipline within his religious societies.

The Congregationalists of New England met at Cambridge, Massachusetts, from 1646 to 1648 to develop a confession of faith. They affirmed substantial agreement with the Westminster Confession—except in the matter of church discipline. In their *Cambridge Platform*, they drafted a much more detailed section ("Of Excommunication and Other Censures") in which they carefully outlined the procedures for the execution of church discipline. It is one of the most thorough and biblical ecclesiastical statements on this subject. The disciplinary actions of the Congregational churches of Massachusetts reflect the place of church discipline in the history of the church in America.[7]

In tracing the practice of church discipline through the history of the church until recent times, it is quite apparent that such corrective confrontation has virtually always had a place in Christian churches. Its neglect today is not consistent with the

---

[7]Emil Oberholzer, Jr., *Delinquent Saints* (New York: AMS Press, Inc., 1968).

rigorous efforts of the past to correct sinners and maintain a pure church.

Francis Schaeffer, in a letter to the editor of *Christianity Today,* expressed his concern over a spirit of accommodation among many evangelical Christians:

> This new step of accommodation to the world spirit about us is rooted in two groups: those who are willing to accommodate to a lower view of Scripture, and those who no longer hold to the third mark of a true church, discipline.[8]

With this accommodation, says Schaeffer, comes "the abandonment of the biblical teaching of the practice of the purity of the visible church." Church discipline has held an important place in the Christian Church throughout history. It is time for that place of importance to be restored.

Sins Requiring Discipline

What sins ought the church recognize as worthy of discipline? I am not aware of any creed or confession which enumerates the sins for which discipline should be applied. The Bible, however, does provide several lists of sins which should serve as a starting point in answering this question. Some believers might fear that such a list of offenses might send the church on a witch hunt. On the contrary, focusing on such scriptural guidelines will encourage those involved in church discipline to deal with specific issues, not merely personality differences.

In the context of church discipline, Paul writes, "But actually, I wrote you not to associate with any so-called brother if he should be an immoral person, or covetous, or an idolater, or a reviler, or a drunkard, or a swindler—not even to eat with such a one" (1 Cor. 5:11). A few verses later he mentions several of these offenses again and adds more to the list: "Or do you not know that the unrighteous shall not inherit the kingdom of God? Do not be deceived; neither fornicators, nor idolaters, nor adulterers, nor effeminate, nor homosexuals, nor thieves, nor covetous, nor drunkards nor revilers nor swindlers, shall inherit the kingdom of God" (1 Cor. 6:9–10). Such activities characterize those who know not the Lord Jesus Christ. A professing believer in-

---

[8]Francis A. Schaeffer, "To the Editor," *Christianity Today* (November 11, 1983), p. 82.

volved in such activities clearly needs confrontation and correction.

In Gal. 5:19–21 Paul provides a list of "deeds of the flesh" which testify that a person is outside the faith and "shall not inherit the kingdom of God." Included are: immorality, impurity, sensuality, idolatry, sorcery, enmities, strife, jealousy, outbursts of anger, disputes, dissensions, factions, envyings, drunkenness, and carousings. The fact that Paul adds ". . . and things like these" indicates the list is suggestive, rather than exhaustive. Therefore, such *kinds* of sins would be worthy of discipline.

A similar list is given by Jesus in His discussion of matters which issue from the heart and consequently defile a person (Mark 7:21, 22). They include: evil thoughts and fornications, thefts, murders, adulteries, deeds of coveting and wickedness, deceit, sensuality, envy, slander, pride, and foolishness.

In 2 Tim. 3:1–5 Paul discusses the kinds of people to avoid in the last days. They include those who are: lovers of self, lovers of money, boastful, arrogant, revilers, disobedient to parents, ungrateful, unholy, unloving, irreconcilable, malicious gossips, without self-control, brutal, haters of good, treacherous, reckless, conceited, and lovers of pleasure rather than lovers of God. In Titus 3:10, he mentions the "factious man" as one who must be rejected if he refuses correction. In Rom. 16:17, he names those who "cause dissensions and hindrances contrary to the teaching which you learned" as individuals to avoid.

Should a church use these biblical texts to formulate a list of offenses requiring discipline? Should discipline be applied to some or all? Paul answers these questions in Gal. 6:1: "Brethren, even if a man is caught in any trespass, you who are spiritual, restore such a one in a spirit of gentleness; looking to yourself, lest you too be tempted." Notice that Paul says "any trespass." He isn't choosy about which sin or offense is involved. This seems to be the attitude of Jesus in Matt. 5:23–24 where he admonishes his listeners to reconcile themselves with offended brothers before participating in worship. He refers to the offense with a general term ("something") rather than precisely specifying it.

Gal. 6:1 and Matt. 5:23–24 appear to indicate that any and all sins are worthy of personal confrontation and correction. Daniel Wray, a pastor and author of *Biblical Church Discipline*, says it well: "All breaches of the biblical standards of doctrine and behavior require some form of discipline."[9] The corrective

---

[9]Daniel E. Wray, *Biblical Church Discipline* (Edinburgh: The Banner of Truth Trust, 1978), p. 8.

action taken will vary according to the reaction of the offender, but known sin requires some response. This does not mean, of course, that church members are going to wear Gestapo uniforms and put each other under surveillance. Rather, as members of the body of Christ, they will recognize their family responsibilities to lovingly challenge and correct one another.

The sins which necessitate church discipline can be divided into four major categories: *violations of Christian love, unity, law, and truth*.[10] Violations of *love* would include private offenses against a brother or sister (cf. Matt. 5:23–24). Violations of Christian *unity* would be divisive actions which destroy the peace of the church (Rom. 16:17; Titus 3:10). Violations of Christian *law* or morality would involve the breaking of such ethical codes and guidelines as are set forth in the Old and New Testaments; the scriptural lists of offenses can help in clearly identifying the unlawful actions or activities. Violations of Christian *truth* would involve the rejection of essential doctrines of the faith—heresy (1 Tim. 6:3–5; Titus 3:10; 2 John 7–11).

The twentieth-century church needs a concentrated injection of David Augsburger's "care-fronting."[11] This is the key to effective relationships in the home, in the church, and in the world, for such confrontation is corrective, not vindictive or personal. It needs to occur as soon after the misbehavior as possible so as to have the greatest influence on future behavior. It requires "speaking the truth in love" (Eph. 4:15).

Does the church today care enough to confront? Jesus did. And His followers must also if Christ's bride is to be kept pure in anticipation of His coming.

---

[10]Ibid., pp. 8–9.
[11]David Augsburger, *Caring Enough to Confront* (Glendale, Calif.: Regal Books, 1973), p. 3.

4

THE STEPS FOR DISCIPLINE—
THE TEACHING OF JESUS

After the purchase of a swing-and-glider set for the children's play area at church, my son and I took on the challenge of assembling the equipment. As we opened the long cardboard carton, we found the parts which we hoped would eventually become a whole—bars, poles, plastic seats, and several large plastic bags full of nuts, bolts and washers. I surveyed the situation and wondered if I would ever be able to put that mess together!

Then I spied a white sheet of paper titled, "Assembly Directions," and I remembered the wise counsel given me by fathers with great experience in assembling children's toys: "When all else fails, read the directions." I unfolded the sheet and followed the manufacturer's instructions. Within a couple of hours the equipment was completely assembled.

Church discipline is sometimes attempted by those who have not taken the time to "read the instructions." The results are disastrous. Not only is the process made more lengthy and painful, but usually the objectives are never realized. The wise course of action would be to follow the directions which Christ, the builder of the church, has provided in Matt. 18:15–17. Here Jesus outlines four basic steps to correction: (1) private reproof, (2) private conference, (3) public announcement, and (4) public exclusion.

Private Reproof

In Matt. 18:5–14 Jesus warns His disciples against the evil of influencing others to sin. In verse 7 He declares, "Woe to the world because of its stumbling blocks! For it is inevitable that stumbling blocks come; but woe to that man through whom the stumbling block comes!" Believers are responsible to avoid situations which may lead others to stumble into sin. Woe to the one who brings spiritual ruin to the life of another!

But suppose you are not the sinner, but the one sinned against? How is a Christian to respond? Having pronounced judgment on those who would lead others to sin, Jesus explains what a believer should do if he has been hurt or wronged by a brother.

The first step is given in verse 15. Jesus declares, "And if your brother sins [against you], go and reprove him in private; if he listens to you, you have won your brother." The offended believer is responsible to arrange a private meeting and confront the brother or sister with the sin.

There has been a good deal of debate as to whether the words "against you" are part of the original Greek Text.[1] They are absent in several important manuscripts (*Codex Vaticanus* and *Codex Sinaiticus*). It is possible that the words "against me" in verse 21 led a scribe or copyist to personalize the matter in verse 15. On the other hand, the omission may have been deliberate in order to render the passage applicable to sin in general. While some important textual tradition lacks the words "against you," Gundry reveals evidence for their originality.[2] The words in the next clause, "between you and him alone" (NASB translates, "in private"), and the next section which speaks about forgiving a brother who has sinned against a brother (18:21–35) favor the originality of "against you."

Whether the words "against you" are in the original text or not, it is clear from Gal. 6:1 that believers have a responsibility to confront sin in general, not just when it is an offense against one's person. Paul says, "Brethren, even if a man is caught in any trespass, you who are spiritual, restore such a one in a spirit of gentleness; looking to yourself, lest you too be tempted." Both Jesus and Paul are calling for believers to involve themselves in the lives of others. They are charging believers to take loving action when a brother or sister is on the road to spiritual disaster.

Jesus says the brother is to be reproved. "Reprove" is a strong word which may mean "to bring to light, expose, convict, or convince someone of something." The word implies a rebuke which brings conviction. With the same word Jesus describes the

---

[1] Bruce M. Metzger, *Textual Commentary on the Greek New Testament* (London: United Bible Societies, 1971), p. 45.

[2] Robert H. Gundry, *Matthew: A Commentary on His Literary and Theological Art* (Grand Rapids: Wm. B. Eerdmans Publishing Co., 1982), p. 367.

ministry of the Holy Spirit in the life of the unbeliever: "And He, when He comes, will convict the world concerning sin, and righteousness, and judgment" (John 16:8). In this context, "reprove" simply means to show someone his fault.

There are many ways in which one can point out a fault. As a teacher I have dealt with students who have not exhibited a teachable spirit or who have been disrespectful in class. As one in authority, I could come down hard on these students and exercise strong measures to deal with the situation. But that is not the biblical way. Paul directs us to "restore such a one in a spirit of gentleness" (Gal. 6:1). Pointing out someone's fault is risky. There is no way of knowing how he will respond. It must be done *gently*, in a way that encourages the person to recognize the error rather than become stubborn and bitter. This is loving, caring confrontation.

As I initiate a personal confrontation of this nature, I first remind myself of how I have failed in the past, even as this brother or sister has. I think of how I was corrected or how I would want to be treated if I slipped into such a situation again. I want to encourage the spiritual growth of this young person, not squash his enthusiasm or destroy his self-esteem. My goal is to bring healing, not throw salt in a wound.

Then, before the confrontation takes place, I bring the matter before the Lord in prayer. I follow Samuel's example: After Israel demanded a king, Samuel first prayed to the Lord, then spoke to the people (1 Sam. 8:6). Bringing the matter before the Lord enables me to deal with any personal bitterness or resentment *before* that personal confrontation takes place.

Finally, when the confrontation occurs, I begin by expressing my genuine appreciation for the good qualities I see in that person's life. I detail these at length to help the person know I am sincerely interested in his spiritual welfare. Then, and only then, do I broach the matter which concerns me.

In some situations the sin is very apparent and there is little or no doubt that the brother or sister has sinned. Usually, however, it is wise in the first confrontation to allow for the possibility that I am misjudging. Perhaps I misunderstand the situation or somehow have the facts wrong. It is wise, therefore, to explain my concern and then ask, "Charles, am I observing this situation correctly?" or, "Is there a misunderstanding that needs to be cleared up?" I sometimes have found, after leaping to a conclusion, that I don't have the facts in order. Many misunderstandings have been cleared up simply by bringing an issue or potential difficulty out in the open. Such loving confrontation usually strengthens my relationship with that person. Even if there is a specific sin involved, most people appreciate that I am concerned enough to risk confronting them.

The first confrontation, of course, must be private. Jesus uses the words "between you and him alone." In other words, I have no right to bring up the matter in public or in conversation with anyone else before I have spoken to that brother or sister in private. This prevents misunderstandings from taking place.

Such a misunderstanding occurred some years ago when I was falsely accused of making an inappropriate comment in class about another teacher. Sadly, the matter came to the attention of the dean before anyone confronted me with the issue personally, so a great misunderstanding transpired. This would have been avoided if I had been approached about it in private first.

In the the last clause of Matt. 18:15, Jesus reveals the potential results of caring confrontation. "If he listens to you, you have won your brother." The word "listens" sometimes connotes more than the idea of merely hearing with the ear. It may take the stronger nuance, "to agree, follow, heed or obey" (John 5:25b; 9:27a; Acts 28:28). That seems to be the sense of the word here and in verse 16. This conclusion is supported by what is an apparent summary of Jesus' instruction on this matter in Luke 17:3—"If your brother sins, rebuke him; and if he repents, forgive him." If the one you have confronted heeds what you say and either clarifies the issue or recognizes the sin and repents of it, that person is saved for usefulness in the body of Christ.

This text makes clear that when we are approached by a fellow member of the body of Christ about any matter, we have the responsibility to *listen*. Listening isn't easy. It requires dropping our defenses and desiring to know the truth. Most of us spend "listening time" planning what we are going to say in defense of our actions! In such cases we must remember that Christ is our Defender, our Advocate (1 John 2:1) and that truth brings spiritual freedom (John 8:32). Don Bubna offers this helpful advice for those who want to be better listeners: "One of the things that has helped me is disciplining myself to listen so carefully that I can summarize to the person what he has said. I ask him to correct my summary so he knows I have really listened."[3]

---

[3]Bubna, "Redemptive Love: The Key to Church Discipline," p. 81.

There has been some debate in the history of the church as to whether there must be a public confession of a sin that has been dealt with privately. Jeschke argues that the church of the first few centuries consistently required persons under discipline to make a public confession.[4] But Matthew's text does not suggest that this is necessary. In fact, it appears from Matthew 18 that whether the confession will be public or private depends upon the stage at which the person responds to admonition.

The general policy would be that sins which have been dealt with privately should not be made public. The only exception would be in the case of a sin which has public consequences. It would be best for the congregation to know that an unmarried woman who is pregnant has repented of the sin and now needs the loving support and encouragement of the church family to help her through the difficult time ahead. It would be best for the congregation to know that the businessman who is under indictment for fraud has repented of the sin and now needs the support and encouragement of the church family as he faces a trial and possible jail sentence. Such matters which will inevitably become public should be revealed to the church family in such a way as to bring loving encouragement to those who have repented of their sins but now face the serious public consequences of their actions.

Private Conference

Many personal offenses and issues of sin can be dealt with adequately at the private, personal level. But what if the brother or sister is unwilling to listen? What if obvious sin is not acknowledged and confessed? Jesus anticipates that such will occasionally be the case. In Matt. 18:16, He says, "But if he does not listen to you, take one or two more with you, so that by the mouth of two or three witnesses every fact may be confirmed." Jesus may be drawing upon the Old Testament requirement that a person could not be convicted of a crime on the basis of a single witness (Deut. 17:6; 19:15; Num. 35:30, cf. 2 Cor.13:1; 1 Tim. 5:19). Several witnesses were required in order to ensure that the testimony was true and unprejudiced.

What purpose, then, do the additional witnesses serve? Possibly they have observed the sin and are thereby able to strengthen

---

[4]Jeschke, *Discipling the Brother*, p. 92.

the rebuke. In legal process, the absence of witnesses or the existence of only one witness makes securing a conviction difficult. The biblical requirement of additional witnesses safeguards the judicial process against false accusation, slander, and wrongful incrimination. In the disciplinary process, those who have observed a sin in the life of a believer are able to strengthen the rebuke by confirming the charges. The witnesses may also serve to bring new objectivity to the situation by helping the truth to surface, and could be called upon to testify if the case comes before the congregation.

Gundry, however, takes a different view:

> Matthew leaves no indication that the one or two others shall have witnessed the sin committed against the one who takes them along. Therefore their going does not have the purpose of establishing the original charge (the truth of which is taken for granted) or of enabling them to act as witnesses before the church in case of a second refusal, but of strengthening the reproof with a view toward restoration.[5]

While the witnesses may serve to bring greater objectivity to the situation, Gundry asserts that their primary purpose is to strengthen the rebuke and thus lead the sinner to repentance. As Hendriksen comments, "It may be easier for two or three persons to succeed in this task than for one."[6]

There is merit to the observation that the truth of the charges is taken for granted, but the very term "witness" implies some kind of observation by eye and ear. While a witness actually may not have been present during the act, he should be able to present evidence beyond reasonable doubt that an act of sin occurred. For example, the witness may not have seen the act of adultery. But observing a married woman entering another man's home late at night may be sufficient evidence, along with other considerations, that a sin or indiscretion has occurred. Even if he has never seen such behavior, if the sinner—during the confrontation—admits his act, the witness has become a bearer of evidence.

Bringing a matter of sin to a brother's attention in the presence of witnesses may seem a threatening or intimidating scene. Yet the purpose is not to threaten or intimidate the sinner into repentance. The intent is to cause the offender to realize the

---

[5]Gundry, *Matthew*, p. 368.
[6]William Hendriksen, *Exposition of the Gospel According to Matthew* (Grand Rapids: Baker Book House, 1973), p. 700.

seriousness of the situation. Bubna assures, "Although moving into the group process is scary, it does improve the attention level."[7]

Public Announcement

The third step in the process of discipline, as set forth by Jesus, is revealed in verse 17: "And if he refuses to listen to them, tell it to the church." The refusal of a sinning brother or sister to acknowledge his sin and repent requires that the matter be made public by bringing it before the church. Up to this point, the disciplinary procedure has taken place in private. But an unresponsive saint requires stronger action.

When Jesus spoke these words, the organized church of Acts and the New Testament epistles did not yet exist (cf. Matt. 16:18). The word "church" (*ecclesia*) refers here to the local body of believers gathered in assembly. Notice that Jesus does not say, "Tell it to the pope, priest, bishop, synod or some church board." He says, "Tell it to the congregation." The congregation is the final court of appeal in such disciplinary matters.

This is not to say that the church leaders (i.e., elders, pastoral staff, or deacons) should not be informed of the action being taken. Indeed, these leaders are probably the most likely ones to serve as witnesses in the second state of discipline—the private conference. But the principle that seems to underlie Jesus' command to bring the matter before the congregation is that believers are members of one body (1 Cor. 12:14–20), and have a responsibility to "care for one another" (1 Cor. 12:25). That loving care for one another must sometimes take the form of discipline.

How should the matter of a sinning saint be presented to the church? Should it appear in the church bulletin or be read with the morning announcements? Should a special business meeting be called to deal with the issue? Since Jesus does not give any specific instruction regarding *how* the matter is to be brought before the church, perhaps we should allow some flexibility here.

One pastor suggests that the names of offenders ought not to be brought before the church except in cases of excommunication. He interprets Jesus' words to mean that the sin is reported ("tell *it*") but the sinner is left anonymous. Therefore, during a

---

[7]Bubna, "Redemptive Love: The Key to Church Discipline," p. 81.

worship service the matter of concern will be brought before the congregation in the form of a statement from the elders. The statement would acknowledge that some persons have been engaging in practices which violate the principles of Scripture. The congregation is informed that the continuation of such activities will require that the elders take disciplinary action in the matter.

Certainly there is nothing wrong with the principle of instructing the congregation as a whole about abstaining from certain activities which the church leaders consider sinful or harmful to believers. Yet the thought of moving from a personal, private confrontation to a general public announcement does not seem to be in keeping with the text of Matthew 18. The whole passage reflects a personal element that is incongruous with a *general* public announcement.

I would suggest that no matter how the case is brought before the church, it should be done in such a way that encourages the congregation to find its role in bringing the brother or sister to repentance. The people must be encouraged to pray for the sinner, to avoid a critical spirit, and to beware of pridefully thinking, *That would never happen to me.* The thrust of such a public announcement should be that God hates sin but loves sinners. And we Christians must share that attitude.

One church which took disciplinary action regarding a pregnant teen-ager set aside a Sunday evening to deal with the matter. The pastor brought a message on Matt. 18:21–35, emphasizing the gracious provision of God's forgiveness, and His requirement that we forgive one another. Then he said there was one in the fellowship who had become involved in a sin and needed the church family's forgiveness. He paused and asked if that person would acknowledge her sin and thus receive the congregation's forgiveness. The girl stood, reported her condition, and acknowledged her wrongdoing. As the service concluded she was received by those present with open arms and many tears.

Public Exclusion

But what if it doesn't work? What if even the public announcement fails to bring the sinner to his senses? There is one final step in the discipline of an impenitent sinner: "And if he refuses to listen even to the church, let him be to you as a Gentile and a tax-gatherer" (Matt. 18:17b).

The word in verse 17 translated "refuses to listen" may have the meaning "to pay no attention to" or "to ignore someone or something." Sometimes an offender will refuse to come before the church to face the charges against him. In that case the church discipline must proceed in his absence. In other cases, the public rebuke, exhortation, or warning is "heard" but goes unheeded. In either case, after the church leaders and congregation unsuccessfully have made every effort to bring the sinner to repentance, they must ostracize the offender from the church fellowship.

The reference to "the gentile and tax-gatherer" is illuminated by the New Testament's first-century Jewish cultural setting. According to the popular religious opinion of Jesus' day, Gentiles were considered as outsiders with regard to the divine blessings promised Israel. A Gentile was not permitted to pass beyond the outer court of the temple into the sanctuary. The penalty for doing so, and thus violating the sanctity of the temple, was death. Tax-gatherers, such as Zacchaeus (Luke 19:2–10), were Jews who collected revenue for the Roman government. They were regarded as traitors because they served Rome at the expense of their countrymen. Often they overcharged people and pocketed the surplus. They represented foreign domination and corruption. Their unenviable, but lucrative, job made them the outcasts of Jewish society (cf. Matt. 9:10; 11:9; 21:31).

What is Jesus saying, then, about unrepentant sinners? He is simply instructing His disciples that they ostracize the impenitent as is the custom with Gentiles and tax-gatherers. In ecclesiastical jargon this is referred to as "excommunication." The word is derived from the Latin *ex* ("out") and *communico* ("share, communicate"). It refers to the cutting off of a person from the church membership, fellowship, or communion. No longer may that person share in the activities and privileges of church membership. Don Bubna offers a practical description of what this means:

> This means that you treat the person as a nonbeliever, because he is not walking as a believer. It means to keep loving him as Jesus loved the publicans and sinners. It means to reach out to him in witness, but not to relate to him as a member of the body of Christ.[8]

As strong as this disciplinary step is, I would hasten to add that it, too, is intended to bring about repentance. Even this most

[8]Ibid., p. 82.

severe step in church discipline should be motivated out of love and fulfilled in a way that encourages repentance and restoration. Excommunication should communicate the message, "We find your present conduct unacceptable to God and this congregation. Our love for you therefore demands that we take action which, though painful, we hope by God's grace will result in your repentance and restoration to us."

Several years ago I was informed that a former student from the seminary at which I teach had been disciplined by his church because of unconfessed, unrepented adultery. He continued in adultery, and eventually divorced his wife and married his lover. As sad and regrettable as this story is, the discipline imposed by the church finally was effective in bringing about repentance and restoration. The man and his present wife came before the church and genuinely confessed their sin and repented of their past adultery, as well as the extreme hurt brought against the man's former wife.

Having recognized the "clear fruits of repentance in the lives of both of them," the church has forgiven them and accepted their confession and repentance in keeping with the instruction of the Scriptures. The church's pastor reports, "There was genuine acceptance on the part of the members." Needless to say, many difficulties remain. One cannot flaunt God's moral standards and expect to avoid the serious consequences of such action. Therefore the church is ministering to the couple through spiritual counsel. Yet discipline did take place, and God was pleased to use such action to bring about the restoration of the sinning saints.

I cannot emphasize enough the need for the congregation's *positive* action in the disciplinary process. Church discipline provides a unique opportunity for believers to show Christ's redeeming and restoring love. The love and acceptance given to a fallen saint will never be forgotten. We must remember that love and acceptance shown to a sinner does not mean being "soft" on sin. The discipline itself acknowledges that the sin is not acceptable, but loving restoration acknowledges that the sinner is.

What are some practical ways to show love? Realize that the church discipline exposes a very private and hidden aspect of a believer's life. Christians therefore must be careful not to pry into personal details that have already been considered by those administering discipline. Sin which has been confessed, forgiven and dealt with by God and His church is "water under the bridge."

There is no reason to give the matter further consideration. Christians should also avoid flippant or insensitive remarks about what has taken place in the life of the offender. Now is the time to "reach out" by showing hospitality, sending an encouraging greeting card, or making a phone call. Christians who have been disciplined need reassurance of the love and acceptance of the church family. This prepares the way to spiritual healing and restoration to fruitful ministry.

5

THE STEPS FOR DISCIPLINE— THE TEACHING OF PAUL

The woman had called me to express concern over a situation which had developed in her church: A lady, an active member in the church, had become pregnant. Not wanting another child, she decided to have an abortion—her second one. She informed several close friends that she was expecting but intended to terminate the pregancy.

The pregnant woman had been confronted by several Christian women who pointed out that abortion involves the destruction of a human life. One woman even offered to adopt the child in order to prevent the destruction of this life. In spite of these attempts to change the woman's mind, she proceeded with the abortion.

Grieving for the little life, a friend took the matter to the pastor. "Shouldn't Betty be confronted with the wrong she has done and be urged to repent?"

The pastor replied, "This is not an issue that the Bible makes clear. I don't want our church to become divided over this matter." He was unwilling even to speak to the woman about the seriousness of using abortion for birth control. He advocated "loving her back into fellowship."

Because of the pastor's unwillingness to address this issue, the offender has never admitted any wrong. And since the incident had become public knowledge, many believers have left the church. The problem is that the ones leaving are those who are sensitive to sin and desire a holy fellowship! The leaven of impurity is permeating this congregation. Things have not changed very much since the first century when Paul had to rebuke the Corinthian believers for tolerating open sin among believers.

Like Jesus, Paul presents some very helpful instruction regarding the matter of church discipline. He acknowledges the same essential steps that Jesus presents in Matt. 18:15–17 and provides some further details regarding the last step of discipline—excommunication.

Preliminary Procedures

Unlike Jesus, the Apostle Paul does not present a systematic, step-by-step procedure for administering church discipline. Yet Paul clearly acknowledges that there are preliminary steps which must be taken before the ultimate discipline of excommunication is administered.

Personal appeal

Paul counsels young Timothy that while there is a place for a strong rebuke (2 Tim. 4:2), on some occasions the best course of action is to offer a personal appeal. Paul writes, "Do not sharply rebuke an older man, but rather appeal to him as a father; to the younger men as brothers, the older women as mothers, and the younger women as sisters, in all purity" (1 Tim. 5:1–2). The personal appeal avoids the harsh, confrontive nature of stronger forms of discipline. The personal appeal involves a coming alongside and offering a correction in a loving, gentle way.

I recently received correction by way of a personal appeal. I had delivered a sermon at a church where I was ministering as a guest. In the context of a message on the value of human life, I spoke of some people whom God had allowed to be "handicapped" for the ultimate purpose of bringing glory to himself (cf. John 9:3). I used "handicapped" several times in the message. After the service, a young woman who worked with such individuals kindly informed me that a less offensive and more appropriate term is "disabled." She informed me that a "handicap" is actually a matter of attitude. "Disabilities" can be overcome. Perhaps the issue seems trivial, but the point is that this younger woman was bold enough to appeal to me, a guest speaker, to change my terminology. I appreciated her helpful instruction and the manner in which it was given. And I am following her advice.

A personal appeal is most appropriate in dealing with a person older than oneself. Several biblical texts stress respect for the elder (cf. Ex. 20:12; Deut. 5:16; Eph. 6:2). Homer Kent comments, "Admonition is necessary for all, but a disrespectful, roughshod assault upon an older man by a minister who is younger merely lays the accuser open to rebuke."[1] The same instruction would apply to one's dealings with an older woman.

Paul emphasizes that the personal appeal reflects the family relationship which is shared by members of the body of Christ. This is seen in the comparisons, "as a father, . . . as brothers, . . . as mothers, . . . as sisters" (1 Tim. 5:1–2). Gentle dealings will often make the offender more inclined to hear and heed the admonition.

Sharp rebuke

When Paul wrote to Titus who was ministering on the island of Crete, he acknowledged that the Cretans "profess to know God, but by their deeds they deny Him" (Titus 1:16). Many were rebellious, deceiving others, upsetting entire families, and ministering only for profit. Paul appeals to one of the well-known Cretan poets, Epimenides (born c. 600 B.C.), who said, "Cretans are always liars, evil beasts, lazy gluttons." Paul admits that this uncomplimentary testimony is true!

What is to be done with such individuals in the church? Paul counsels Titus, "For this cause reprove them severely that they may be sound in the faith" (Titus 1:13). The word "reprove" is the same word that Jesus uses in Matt. 18:15 as He gives directions regarding the first step in dealing with a sinning brother. It is a strong word which may be translated, "bring to light," "expose," "convict" or "convince." The word implies a rebuke which brings conviction. The word appears elsewhere in similar contexts (2 Tim. 4:2; Titus 2:15).

Commanding Titus to use such a rebuke, Paul appends the adverb "severely," which is derived from a verb meaning "to cut off." It suggests abruptness, curtness, or in this context, sharpness or severity.

Paul is acknowledging a time and place for strong words of reproof in dealing with an unrepentant sinning saint. Such a reprimand should involve telling the offender in specific terms what he or she did wrong. Following the suggestion of Blanchard and Johnson for their "one minute reprimand," tell the offender

---

[1]Homer A. Kent, *The Pastoral Epistles* (Chicago: Moody Press, 1958), p. 168.

how you *feel* about the wrong which was committed.[2] This serves to drive the rebuke home to the heart and emotions so that change can issue from the heart and not be outward only. Then tell the offender the consequences of continuing such behavior, reminding him you value him and care for him, and therefore don't want him to suffer these consequences.

The need for witnesses

In his teaching on church discipline, Jesus instructs that if the offender fails to respond to a private reproof, then a private conference should be held in which "two or three" witnesses are invited to participate (Matt. 18:15–16; cf. Deut. 17:6). The primary purpose of such witnesses would not be to establish the truth of the charge, though they might bring new objectivity to the situation. Instead, the witnesses would be present to strengthen the rebuke, thus directing the sinner to repentance.

In accordance with the instructions given by Jesus, the Apostle Paul recognizes the need for witnesses in bringing a charge or accusation against a church elder. He writes to young Timothy, "Do not receive an accusation against an elder except on the basis of two or three witnesses" (1 Tim. 5:19). In addition to strengthening the rebuke, the context seems to suggest that Paul is concerned that the elder not be subjected to slander or personal attack. The requirement of testimony from witnesses would serve as a precautionary measure against unjust and unverified accusations.

While Paul's instructions offer counsel concerning Timothy's dealings with church officers, these words would be applicable to church discipline in general. Paul is undoubtedly drawing upon the teaching of Jesus regarding church discipline and making a specific application of the principles in dealing with elders. He clearly has borrowed from Jesus' teaching regarding the need for witnesses in the process of confronting and correcting a sinning saint. Their purpose is not to appear at a public trial testifying against the offender, but rather to call the sinner to accountability and encourage genuine repentance from wrongdoing.

---

[2]Kenneth Blanchard and Spencer Johnson, *The One Minute Manager* (New York: Berkley Books, 1983), p. 59.

The Public Censure

If the preliminary step of church discipline fails to accomplish its objective, Paul recognizes that, according to the instructions of Jesus, the matter must go before the church (cf. Matt. 18:17). Concerning the matter of disciplining elders, Paul writes, "Those who continue in sin, rebuke in the presence of all, so that the rest also may be fearful of sinning" (1 Tim. 5:20). The word "rebuke" is the same word used by Jesus in Matt. 18:15 and Paul in Titus 1:13. The rebuke is designed to expose, convict, and convince the sinner of the need to repent.

The public nature of the rebuke is not simply intended to put heavy peer pressure on the offender. Nor is it meant to shame, humiliate, or punish a sinning saint. Rather, the rebuke before the church should let the congregation know that what this member has done (or is doing) does not meet with the approval of God or the church leaders. Any such public announcement should not be just an announcement of the fact of the sin, but an expression of grief and concern over the saint who has fallen into sin and is so blinded and hardened as to be unrepentant.

Paul did not simply write about the place for a public rebuke. He applied this procedure as a teacher in the church at Antioch. While Paul was ministering at Antioch on the Orontes (Acts 13:1), Peter came for a visit. Peter had learned from his vision and his experience with Cornelius in Acts 10 that he "should not call any man unholy or unclean" (Acts 10:28), so at Antioch he was enjoying dining with Gentile believers. But when certain Jewish Christians from Jerusalem arrived, Peter "began to withdraw and hold himself aloof, fearing the party of the circumcision" (Gal. 2:13). This led other believing Jews to withdraw and avoid having fellowship with the Gentile believers.

What was Paul to do about this hypocrisy? Although Galatians tells us nothing about Paul's attempt to correct Peter privately, it is unlikely he would have ignored the preliminary steps in discipline—unless he did so intentionally because of the seriousness of the sin or the position of leadership Peter held in the church. Either way, Paul "opposed him to his face, because he stood condemned" (Gal. 2:11). Peter was being inconsistent. He knew that the Gentile believers were accepted by God, but because of peer pressure from influential Jewish believers, he played the role of a scrupulous Jew, avoiding contact with Gentiles.

In Gal. 2:14 Paul tells us he had to confront Peter publicly to correct this sinning saint. "But when I saw that they were not straightforward about the truth of the gospel, I said to Cephas [Peter] in the presence of all, 'If you, being a Jew, live like the Gentiles and not like the Jews, how is it that you compel the Gentiles to live like Jews?' " Although Peter had not been *teaching* that Gentiles should adopt Jewish customs, his *actions* implied they should.

Although Paul does not inform the Galatians how Peter responded to the public censure, he must have responded positively. Later at the Jerusalem Council Peter stood up and defended Paul's position that Gentile believers not be required to adopt Jewish ordinances (cf. Acts 15:7–11). Obviously, Paul's disciplinary action against Peter's hypocrisy was effective in restoring an apostle who had strayed.

Excommunication

I am sure that Paul was grateful for Peter's positive response to the public censure at Antioch, but what if Peter had failed to respond? What if Peter had refused to receive this correction? Jesus had instructed His disciples that there was one final step in church discipline designed to restore the sinning saint. That step is excommunication—the cessation of church membership, fellowship, and sharing together in worship at the Lord's table (Matt. 18:17). Paul had to direct the churches at Thessalonica and Corinth to take such action against sinning saints.

Discipline by avoidance

Many of the Corinthian believers had apparently been strongly influenced by Greek dualism, which held that the body, belonging to the world of matter, was an evil burden and a hindrance to the soul. The soul, belonging to the immaterial world, was good and the essence of reality. Believing that only the soul possessed immortality (cf. 1 Cor. 15), some Corinthians concluded that what they did with their physical bodies was of little eternal consequence. "The body has appetites that should be satisfied," argued the Corinthians (6:12). Paul refutes such arguments by pointing out that "the body is not for immorality, but for the Lord" (6:13). Since the body is destined to be resurrected and preserved for all eternity (6:14), Christians are admonished not to participate in immorality or associate with a professing Christian who is engaging in immoral practices.

In 1 Cor. 5:9 Paul reminds the Corinthian believers of his previous instructions regarding the matter of church discipline: "I wrote you in my letter not to associate with immoral people." Lest his readers think that Paul intends for them to avoid any contact with unbelievers, Paul clarifies the matter in verse 11: "But actually, I wrote to you not to associate with any so-called brother if he should be an immoral person, or covetous, or an idolater, or a reviler, or a drunkard, or a swindler—not even to eat with such a one." In other words, they were to shun only a person who claimed to be Christian but did not live as one.

A different situation existed in the church at Thessalonica. The problem there was not immorality, but disorder. Apparently some false teachers had persuaded the Thessalonian believers that the "day of the Lord" had come (2 Thess. 2:2). Believing the Lord's return to be quite near, they had gone to the extreme of giving up their jobs and living idle, disorderly, undisciplined lives (2 Thess. 3:12).

Paul responds to this situation by pointing out that such disorderly conduct does not follow his instruction or his personal example (2 Thess. 3:6–10)—Paul had worked "night and day" while ministering at Thessalonica to avoid being a financial burden on the church. In dealing with these disorderly, undisciplined saints, Paul instructs the Thessalonians to "avoid every brother who leads an unruly life" (2 Thess. 3:6). In verse 14 he declares, "And if anyone does not obey our instruction in this letter, take special note of that man and do not associate with him, so that he may be put to shame." Anyone who did not honor the disciplinary measures would also be subject to discipline!

The expression "do not associate with" is found only in 1 Cor. 5:11 and 2 Thess. 3:14. It means, quite literally, "not to mix yourselves up together with." Paul is apparently forbidding fellowship and fraternization with those who profess to know Christ but whose actions deny the genuineness of their profession.

This instruction broaches the matter of avoidance, referred to in some churches as "shunning." Two questions must be considered with regard to this subject. First, is this a form of discipline which is to be distinguished from excommunication? Second, to what degree should the command for disassociation be applied?

Some would suggest that Paul is speaking here of a mild form of discipline which falls short of the final step mentioned by Jesus in Matt. 18:17. Many have taken it to refer to a form of ostracism within the church prior to the step for full excommunication. This view is based on instances in other epistles in which Paul mentions the principle of avoidance. For instance, he commands the Romans to "keep your eye on those who cause dissensions and hindrances contrary to the teaching which you learned, and turn away from them" (Rom. 16:17). Also, he instructs Timothy to "avoid such men" as those "holding to a form of godliness, although they have denied its power" (2 Tim. 3:5).

In the context of 1 Cor. 5, however, it seems clear Paul is thinking of that one final step of discipline Jesus specified in Matt. 18:17. This is evident from Paul's final words in verse 13: "Remove the wicked man from among yourselves." To "not associate" with an unrepentant offender is a logical and necessary result of dismissing that person from the assembly of the saints. Such a removal will prevent the offender from enjoying any Christian fellowship or ministry of encouragement by the brethren until he adequately deals with his sin. There seems to be no place, then, for the idea that Christians are to ostracize a brother or sister remaining *within* the church. This would be inconsistent with the nature of fellowship which is an essential aspect of church life (Acts 2:42).

But what exactly does the command to "not associate" with the immoral Christian mean? Some have proposed that the command is absolute, that there should be absolutely no contact between believers and an offender under discipline. Menno Simons, for example, held that the rule applied even in the context of marriage and family relationships. In early Dutch Mennonitism, couples were interrogated at their wedding in the presence of the congregation as to their willingness to shun one's spouse in case he should fall under the ban; an affirmative answer was required.[3] Others have taken the command as instruction to avoid unnecessary social interchange with a sinning saint. In other words, a wife may speak to her husband, and an employee to his boss, about necessary matters, but social interchange in a positive, edifying, encouraging manner must be avoided.

This latter viewpoint not only is more consistent with the spirit of correction, rather than punishment, but it fits better with what Paul says in 2 Thess. 3:14. There the expression "do not

---

[3] Jeschke, *Discipling the Brother*, p. 196–97.

associate" is used in a context in which *some* association or contact is commanded. Paul writes, "And if anyone does not obey our instruction in this letter, take special note of that man and do not associate with him, so that he may be put to shame. And yet do not regard him as an enemy, but admonish him as a brother" (2 Thess. 3:14, 15).

Paul instructs that the believer is not "to associate" with a sinning brother, but is to "admonish" him. Clearly, the avoidance involves communication of some sort. The communication would not be of the warm, friendly, "buddy-buddy" type, but it would be cordial. It would be a statement to the offender that he or she is standing outside the fellowship of the church and is urged to repent. Biblical avoidance must communicate that the offender has forsaken the way of Christian discipleship. At the same time it must communicate the message that full restoration is offered on the basis of confession and repentance.

In his insightful discussion on avoidance, Jeschke offers these helpful words:

> . . . avoidance is that kind of circumspect relationship with an excommunicated individual which brings home to him the truth about his spiritual condition and does not permit him to escape into self-deception. It means refusing to pretend that a person is a Christian after he has ceased to be one. It means respecting his decision and honestly treating him once more like a person of the world.[4]

Paul instructs believers *not* to continue intimate and personal association with one who is undergoing church discipline lest the church think the discipline was of no consequence and lest the offender think the church wasn't serious about the excommunication.

Deliverance over to Satan

In 1 Cor. 5 Paul rebukes the believers for not following his instructions (1 Cor. 5:9) to discipline a man involved in an incestuous marriage with his stepmother. He therefore takes the matter into his own hands, exercising his apostolic authority to initiate church discipline. He declares in verse 5: "I have decided to deliver such a one to Satan for the destruction of his flesh, that his spirit may be saved in the day of the Lord Jesus." Many

---

[4]Ibid., p. 129.

in the history of the church have viewed this discipline as a step beyond excommunication—a more severe form of punishment than that which Jesus details in Matt. 18:17. There are two crucial issues in the verse: the meaning of "deliver over to Satan" and of "destruction of the flesh."

What does Paul mean "to deliver such a one to Satan"? The expression occurs elsewhere only in 1 Tim. 1:20 where Paul says that he had delivered Hymeneus and Alexander unto Satan, so they might learn not to blaspheme. The expression in 1 Cor. 5:9 seems to answer to the words in verse 2: ". . . in order that the one who had done this deed might be removed from your midst." To deliver one to Satan involves a removal from the church.

Satan is recognized as "the ruler of this world" (John 12:31) and "the god of this world" (2 Cor. 4:4). The Apostle John says, "We know that we are of God, and the whole world lies in the power of the evil one" (1 John 5:19). To be removed from the church is to be delivered into the "domain of darkness" (Col. 1:13) where Satan holds sway. To be in the realm of Satan is to be more vulnerable, exposed to his schemes, to the attacks and wiles from which a Christian can be protected.

Destruction of the flesh

The most difficult interpretive issue is the meaning of "the destruction of the flesh." Many commentators suggest Paul has physical suffering in mind. The "flesh" would be understood to refer to a person's physical body. The "destruction of the flesh" would refer, then, to physical suffering, perhaps even death, designed to bring the offender to repentance. True, a link between sin and suffering can be seen in such passages as John 5:14, 1 Cor. 11:30 and James 5:13–16, but it is difficult to see how excommunication could assist in bringing on physical affliction or death.

Others have argued that the word "flesh" must be understood in a non-physical sense—the subduing of the old nature that resides in a man's inner being. Paul's delivering the offender over to Satan would be designed to purify him by destroying his sinful lusts. The major difficulty with this viewpoint, however, is that we would expect the influence of Satan's realm to stimulate the activity of the flesh rather than subdue it.

In an insightful article, Anthony Thiselton develops the viewpoint that the "flesh" (sarx) refers here to the mental attitude of "self-satisfaction."[5] According to Thiselton, we must interpret verse 5 in light of Paul's previous usages of "flesh" in 1 Cor. (cf. 3:1–3). Paul's evaluation of the Corinthian church as being "puffed up" and boastful (5:2,6) indicates that the manifestation of the "flesh" in 1 Cor. 5:5 is one of attitude. Such self-sufficiency, self-direction, and selfishness are the basis for many manifestations of sin. In a thorough examination of Thiselton's viewpoint, S. Kenneth Wilmot writes:

> Though God is not pleased with sexual immorality, greed, idolatry, slander, drunkenness and swindling, He is more burdened with the attitude that results in these activities. Such a mindset as "self-satisfaction" stands in antithesis to the very character of God.[6]

Both the context of 1 Cor. 5:5 and usage of *sarx* in the epistle argue strongly for the viewpoint that Paul intends the discipline to destroy the self-sufficient, carnal attitude of the unrepentant offender. The purpose of this discipline is reflected in the clause, "that his spirit may be saved in the day of the Lord Jesus." In this context, the word "spirit" probably refers not to man's immaterial being, but to his inner self or person (cf. 2 Cor. 2:13). The man who faces the Lord with such a history of selfish and sinful action will have little to glory in on the day of evaluation (1 Cor. 3:10–15; 2 Cor. 5:10). But if the corrective measures work, then the repentant sinner will look forward to a good evaluation at the judgment seat of Christ.

"Situational" Discipline

Because church discipline is designed to be corrective rather than punitive, the sinner's situation, spiritual sensitivity and state of repentance must be considered as church discipline is exercised. This is not to suggest that sometimes we blink at sin and other times we don't. Believers and church leaders must always acknowledge sin as sin and exert themselves to correct a sinning saint. But the discipline I give my children depends in large measure upon their attitude and responsiveness to my correc-

---

[5]Anthony C. Thiselton, "The Meaning of *sarx* in 1 Corinthians 5:5: A Fresh Approach in the Light of Logical and Semantic Factors," *Scottish Journal of Theology* 28 (1973): 204–228.

[6]S. Kenneth Wilmot, "A Contextual and Exegetical Interpretation of 1 Corinthians 5:5–"The Destruction of the Flesh" (Th.M. Thesis, Western Conservative Baptist Seminary, 1979), p. 134.

tion. I am suggesting that this principle be taken into account in administering church discipline.

There is evidence in Paul's writings which suggests he was sensitive to situations requiring discipline and did not try to match every situation with a previously determined, airtight procedure. In dealing with the undisciplined Thessalonians who had quit their jobs and were minding everyone's business but their own, Paul instructs, "If anyone will not work, neither let him eat" (2 Thess. 3:10). Paul does not question the integrity of those who are unable to work and provide for themselves. But by condemning those who are unwilling to work, he prohibits misguided charity. As D. Edmond Heibert comments, "He is insisting that such deliberate loafers must not be supported out of a false sense of charity."[7] Those who refuse to work should be allowed to go hungry. The experience of going to bed on an empty stomach will motivate most people to return to work!

Refusing to feed loafers who are able to provide for themselves appears to be a creative form of discipline. Most likely, a personal confrontation and private conference preceded this measure by Paul. But this example seems to suggest the possibility of allowing the situation to dictate, at least in some measure and on some occasions, the kind of discipline that is imposed.

Perhaps some situations require corrective action, but full excommunication would not be in order. This may be the way to deal with an alcoholic or drug abuser. Such a person might, as a condition for continued church membership, be required to begin treatment for his dependency. A heretic might be required to complete a correspondence course in theology. Refusal to respond and follow the required steps would result in the final step of discipline—excommunication.

Chuck Swindoll, on the matter of church discipline, writes in a letter, ". . . I frequently find myself altering what was previously done due to unique situations." He later notes, "Some general things can be given as guidelines, but an attempt to categorize and compartmentalize our reactions is much more complex." These are significant observations. The steps for church discipline should be regarded as *general* guidelines. Leave room for

---

[7]D. Edmond Hiebert, *The Thessalonian Epistles* (Chicago: Moody Press, 1971), p. 344.

the wise counsel of the church leaders. Leave room for the leading of the Holy Spirit. In carrying out biblical church discipline, don't ignore the situation, spiritual sensitivity, and special needs of the brother or sister in need of correction.

6
THE AUTHORITY FOR DISCIPLINE

As a parent I have authority over the lives of my children. This authority means that John, Elisabeth, and Laura have the responsibility of obeying my instructions. Failure to do so requires me to mete out discipline. When I say, "John, park your bicycle and wash your hands for dinner," I expect him to respond quickly and without argument because he recognizes my authority. A failure to recognize my authority will result in disobedience and therefore discipline.

As a seminary professor I have academic authority over the students taking my classes. When I require an assignment to be completed on a certain date, I expect the assignment to be turned in on time. Students do their best to fulfill my expectations and thus avoid the penalty attached to late papers.

But what about the church? The biblical guidelines for the exercise of discipline imply that the local church has authority over its members. From where is that authority derived? From the Bible? From the church constitution? From the elected officers? After giving instructions regarding the steps for church discipline, Jesus speaks to the matter of authority for church discipline. He declares in Matt. 18:18–20 that *God* has given the church authority to exercise corrective discipline:

> Truly I say to you, whatever you shall bind on earth shall have been bound in heaven; and whatever you loose on earth shall have been loosed in heaven. Again I say to you, that if two of you agree on earth about anything that they may ask, it shall be done for them by My Father who is in heaven. For where two or three have gathered together in My name, there I am in their midst.

The Power of the Keys

After acknowledging the truth of Peter's confession, "Thou art the Christ, the Son of the living God" (Matt. 16:16), Jesus begins to reveal His plan for building the church. In the context of that discussion, He tells Peter, "I will give you the keys of the kingdom of heaven; and whatever you shall bind on earth shall have been bound in heaven, and whatever you shall loose on earth shall have been loosed in heaven" (Matt. 16:19). Later, in Matt. 18:20, Jesus repeats the essence of this statement. Jesus' use of the word "truly" (literally *amen*) sets the statement in the form of a solemn declaration. He leaves off the reference to the "keys of the kingdom," but certainly the concept of the keys lies at the root of the power to "bind" and "loose."

The concept of the keys is well-illustrated in Isa. 22:22 where the Lord promises to "set the key of the house of David" on the shoulder of Eliakim, an official in the court of Hezekiah. The Lord then declares, "When he opens no one will shut, when he shuts no one will open." In ancient times, a house steward carried the keys of his master's house and bore the responsibility for its administration, including opening and shutting the door. The exercise of authority was associated with the possession of the house key. The key, therefore, became a symbol of authority. In Rev. 1:18, Christ is seen to have "the keys of death and of Hades." The possession of the "keys" suggests Christ's sovereign authority over death and Hades.

In Matt. 16:18 Peter is given the "keys" which represent his administrative authority in relationship to God's kingdom program. In Matt. 18:20 Jesus switches from the singular pronoun (*soi*) to the plural (*humin*, "you") and thus extends to all His disciples the authority He first delegated to Peter "as a representative disciple."[1]

Some would suggest that the authority to "bind" and "loose" rests only with Peter and the other eleven apostles. But as Lenski points out, this overlooks the fact that Jesus addresses the Twelve here "not in an official capacity, but as members of his church."[2] The general nature of the instruction is revealed by the words, "And if your brother sins" (18:15). Certainly Jesus does not intend His instruction to apply only to sinning apostles. I conclude

---

[1]Gundry, *Matthew*, p. 369.
[2]R.C.H. Lenski, *The Interpretation of St. Matthew's Gospel* (Minneapolis: Augsburg Publishing House, 1961), p. 704.

with Lenski that the authority symbolized by the keys "has been entrusted to no special order of men but to the entire church."[3]

The terms for binding and loosing reflect language used by the rabbis when making decisions regarding the application of a particular law.[4] In making decisions they would either impose the obligation of the law ("bind") or remove the obligation of the law ("loose"). By these Rabbinic declarations, certain activities were either prohibited or permitted. This terminology was also used by the rabbis in a judicial sense to declare a person free from or liable to punishment.

Drawing upon this Jewish background, Jesus gives to the church, represented by the disciples, the authority to "bind" and "loose." The church exercises its authority to "bind" when it imposes discipline on an unrepentant sinner. The immediate context (v. 17) suggests that the "binding" applies primarily to the excommunication of the sinning saint. The power to "bind" and "loose" is essentially the authority to administer corrective discipline in the local assembly of believers. The church exercises its authority to "loose" when it forgives and restores a repentant sinner to full fellowship.

Some debate the grammatical meaning of the words for binding and loosing in Matt. 16:19 and 18:18. Grammatical analysis reveals these words to be periphrastic future perfects. Some versions translate them as simple futures, "shall be bound" and "shall be loosed." Others translate "shall have been bound" and "shall have been loosed." This issue is quite significant. As simple futures, the words of Jesus mean that God has committed himself to ratify the decisions of the church. He will endorse in heaven what the church determines on earth. While this view is possible, it appears to involve an unlikely delegation of divine authority in which God actually subjects himself to the authority of the church instead of exercising sovereignty over it.

A more likely and grammatically defensible option is to translate the verbs "shall have been bound" and "shall have been loosed." This viewpoint is defended in detail by the eminent Greek grammarian, J. R. Mantey, who, with H. E. Dana, authored *A Manual Grammar of the Greek New Testament*. On the basis of his thorough study and research, Mantey asserts that the verbs in

---

[3]Ibid.
[4]Alfred Edersheim, *The Life and Times of Jesus the Messiah*, one volume edition (Grand Rapids: Wm. B. Eerdmans Publishing Co., 1971), ii. 85.

Matt. 16:18 and 18:20 must be translated literally, "shall have been bound" and "shall have been loosed." "No longer," he writes, "are there grounds to claim that in general clauses the perfect may be translated as a future."[5]

According to Mantey's interpretation, in the matter of "binding" and "loosing," the church may so be led by the Spirit of Christ in her midst (cf. 18:20) that the church's decisions reflect the very will of God in heaven. This is not a case of the church merely ratifying God's decision. Rather, the church in union with Christ, her head, makes decisions which are in fact the will of God.

What decisions does Jesus have in mind that the church share in? Some insist the passage refers to the priest's authority to forgive sin. Yet Scripture is quite clear that God alone possesses such authority (cf. Mark 2:1–12). Others believe that Peter used his "keys" to open the church to the Jews (Acts 2), the Samaritans (Acts 8) and the Gentiles (Acts 10). But these views do not fit with the discussion of church discipline. The context in Matt. 18:18 reveals the meaning of the authority given by Christ to the church. The context, of course, is church discipline. Jesus is saying to His disciples that when they exercise church discipline—correcting sinners and forgiving the repentant—such decisions will reflect the will of God in heaven.

The Priority of Prayer

In verse 19 Jesus gives the secret of making right decisions when called upon to exercise church discipline. He declares, "Again I say to you, that if two of you agree on earth about anything that they may ask, it shall be done for them by My Father who is in heaven." This verse, as Matt. 21:22, is often viewed as a general promise to answer the corporate prayers of God's people. But note the context. Jesus is instructing His disciples on the matter of church discipline. Here He is saying that those who prayerfully seek God's wisdom in exercising discipline may have confidence that the decisions they make reflect the will of God in heaven.

The instruction in verse 19 is set in the form of a conditional statement ("if"). This suggests that agreement is a prerequisite

---

[5]Julius Robert Mantey, "Distorted Translations in John 20:23; Matthew 16:18–19 and 18:18," *Review and Expositor* 78 (Summer 1981): 415.

to having the prayer answered positively. The verb "agree" suggests the idea of coming to agreement by talking over a matter. This means that plenty of interaction and discussion is necessary in formulating the prayer request. The figure "two" is not to suggest a low level of participation in such a prayer ministry. The number "two" comes from verse 16, "take one or two more with you." At the second level of confrontation (18:16), two believers may be sufficient to deal with the matter. But if the sinner is unrepentant and the matter is brought before the church, a much larger number would be involved. The point is that full agreement—whether the prayer group be large or small—is essential to answered prayer regarding church discipline.

Instead of making decisions on the basis of a majority vote (19 "for" and 17 "against"), Jesus is setting forth a principle of decision-making based on consensus and unanimity. This is especially important in matters relating to church discipline, for disagreement on such matters will result in dissension, internal strife, and criticism of leaders.

The "anything that they may ask" ought not be interpreted as a *carte blanche*. The promise of answered prayer must be understood within the context of the passage. Jesus is giving instruction regarding church discipline. The promise given here by Jesus is that God will provide wisdom, guidance, and power for decision-making to the church that is united in its prayers regarding matters of church discipline. Robert Cook comments, "The point is, when there is prayerful counsel together following God's guidelines, the Father will stand with you."[6]

The Presence of Christ

In verse 20 Jesus explains why united prayer will be effective: "For where two or three have gathered together in My name, there I am in their midst." Jesus assures His disciples that even when as few as two or three believers gather together as Christians, He is spiritually present in their midst. This truth applies to the situation of discipline, but is not limited to it. It is a basic principle which gives validity to the preceding instructions.

The reference to two or three does not suggest that anytime a small group of believers gathers a church is suddenly formed.

---

[6]W. Robert Cook, "Biblical Concepts of the Discipline of Church Leaders," an unpublished paper read at the Southwest Regional meetings of CBA of A (October 1975), p. 24.

The point is that Christ is present among even the smallest group gathered. He is surely present with a larger group gathered in His name.[7] The mention of the two or three suggests that disciplinary matters need not be made public knowledge. Only a refusal to heed the first and second reproof would result in the matter being brought before the whole church.

What does it mean to gather in Jesus' "name"? In the Jewish culture people were often named or renamed on the basis of a notable character trait. Barnabas, for example, was given the name "son of encouragement" (Acts 4:36) in recognition of his ability to console and encourage. James and John were given the name "sons of thunder" (Mark 3:17), perhaps in view of their fiery emotions (cf. Luke 9:54–56). The name came to represent the person—his character, reputation, and attributes. To gather in Jesus' name, then, is to gather on the basis of His person and work, accepting the meaning and implications of His name (cf. 10:41–42).

Although Jesus never appears to have used the name "Immanuel" (God with us), here that prophetic name given in Isa. 7:14 becomes very meaningful. The name reflects the deity of Christ. As God was with His people in the person of Christ, so Jesus declares that He is in the midst of those who gather in His name. Christ's spiritual presence provides the reason for the heavenly Father's answering our prayers. In Gundry's words, "How could the Father refuse those who prayed gathered in the name of his Son and blessed with the presence of his Son?"[8]

The Use of Christ's Authority

The Apostle Paul appealed to the authority of Jesus in instances where he was involved in church discipline. He writes, "In the name of our Lord Jesus, . . . I have decided to deliver such a one to Satan. . ." (1 Cor. 5:4, cf. 2 Thess. 3:6,12).

In the biblical period, because a person's name represented his character or attributes, his name stood for his total person, for whatever authority was his. Biblically, therefore, to take action "in the name of" someone is to act on his behalf and on his authority. The expression "Stop in the name of the law!" means, "Stop on the basis of my appeal to the authority of the law."

[7]Ibid.
[8]Gundry, *Matthew*, p. 370.

The authority for church discipline does not reside in any one person, administrative body or office. The authority lies with Christ. It is only on the basis of Christ's authority, and the name which represents that authority, that the church is able to exercise discipline.

All authority in heaven and on earth has been delegated by the Father to Jesus Christ. And in the area of church discipline, Christ has delegated His authority to the local assembly of believers. Christians are given Christ's authority to make binding decisions in dealing with unrepentant sinning saints. Since discipline is on the basis of Christ's authority, it ought to be Christ-like—gentle, loving and with a view to restoration. Such disciplinary actions must result from united opinion and fervent prayer. This assures the spiritual presence of Christ in the local assembly, and thus assures that the church's decision will be God's.

In the area of discipline, God will accomplish through the church His will in heaven. What an encouragement to know that God will direct the church in these matters! What a challenge to be so led by the Spirit of Christ that God's decision will be carried out.

7
THE PURPOSE OF DISCIPLINE

Many people fail to make a clear distinction between punishment and discipline, and there is a very significant difference between these two concepts. Punishment is designed to execute *retribution* for a wrong done. Discipline, on the other hand, is designed to encourage the *restoration* of one involved in wrongdoing. Punishment is designed primarily to avenge a wrong and assert justice. Discipline is designed primarily as a corrective for the one who has failed to live according to the standards of the church and/or society.

Shortly after midnight on September 6, 1983, Jimmy Lee Gray entered the gas chamber at the state penitentiary in Parchman, Mississippi, and was executed for the rape and murder of a three-year-old girl. Although Gray had become a Christian in 1977 while awaiting trial, the state of Mississippi determined that the death sentence was proper for one who had committed such a violent and costly crime. That's punishment.

Some time ago a member of a large urban church began making false accusations about the pastor. When confronted by the pastor about his lying and gossiping, the man was quite unresponsive to the rebuke. Eventually the matter was brought before the board of deacons. When challenged by the church leaders as to his false accusations and gossiping, the offender insisted on justifying himself in spite of the overwhelming evidence against him. Finally, a special meeting of the church was convened at which the deacons explained the situation and the member in question was given a chance to respond. The congregation then voted to dismiss the man from church membership. That's discipline. The action taken by the church was not designed to hurt, but to heal. The church's firm discipline was intended to turn the sinner from his way and restore him to fellowship with Christ, the pastor and the church.

Luis Palau presents a sound biblical perspective on church discipline when he points out that discipline is not carried out to punish, but "to awaken people to their sin." He adds that church discipline "is not carried out in cruelty to destroy, but rather in love to produce conviction, sorrow, repentance, and restoration."[1] The church has not been entrusted by God with the responsibility of executing judgment on errant saints. That is God's business. "Vengeance is *Mine*, I will repay, says the Lord" (Rom. 12:19). ". . . fornicators and adulterers *God* will judge" (Heb. 13:4). But God has entrusted the church with the authority and responsibility to carry out discipline. As an essential aspect of discipleship, discipline's purpose is always to help, heal, and restore a wayward saint. Several biblical texts provide insight into this subject.

To Turn About—2 Thess. 3:14

In his concluding comments of his second Thessalonian epistle, Paul gives teeth to the matter of obedience: "And if anyone does not obey our instruction in this letter, take special note of that man and do not associate with him, so that he may be put to shame" (2 Thess. 3:14). The last clause of the verse makes clear that the discipline of disassociation has a definite purpose.

The Greek word *entrepo*, translated "be put to shame," is derived from the word *trepo*, meaning "to turn or direct someone or something." With the preposition *en* ("in"), *entrepo* means "to turn about" or "to turn in." The word may convey the sense of inward reflection ("turn in") which *may* result in shame if one's conduct is in question. While *entrepo* may bear the meaning "put to shame" in certain contexts (cf. 1 Cor. 4:14), here it appears that Paul's concern is to bring about repentance—a genuine turnabout in character and conduct. This seems to be Paul's focus in Titus 2:8 where the word appears again. If the primary objective of the disciplinary action were to shame the offender, the verb *aischuno* (or one of its close relatives), meaning "to be ashamed," would probably have served Paul's purpose better in that it would have left no doubt as to Paul's intended meaning.

The discipline Paul advises in this passage, therefore, is not designed to humiliate and disgrace the fallen saint, but to stim-

---

[1]Luis Palau, "Discipline in the Church," *Discipleship Journal* (Issue 16, 1983), p. 18.

ulate the brother or sister to do some serious inward reflection and "be turned about" from sin.

To Produce Healthy Faith—Titus 1:13

In Titus 1 Paul offers his disciple and fellow worker on Crete wise advice on how to deal with the disorderly teachers in the church. Having described the true character and conduct of the Cretans (Titus 1:10–12), Paul instructs Titus, "For this cause reprove them severely that they may be sound in the faith" (Titus 1:13).

The present tense of the verb "reprove" suggests that one confrontation may not suffice. Paul is actually saying, "Keep on reproving." Persistence in correcting the brother or sister is required for success. The word "severely," or "sharply," means "cut as with a knife." A severe rebuke may be necessary but it must always be done with a spirit of gentleness (cf. Gal. 6:1).

The purpose of the reproof is "that they may be sound in the faith." The expression "be sound" may be translated "be in good health" (cf. 3 John 2), and the verb is used in a metaphorical sense to refer to sound doctrine. Paul's concern is that the disorderly teachers be corrected and that their teaching become sound—"healthy"—for the body of Christ. Paul doesn't throw the problem-people out of the church. He instead admonishes Titus to take firm steps to restore them to a healthy, wholesome teaching ministry.

To Encourage Spiritual Healing—Heb. 12:10–13

In Heb. 12:4–13 the writer of the epistle sets forth the loving motives and beneficial results of God's loving discipline of His own. Although I focused at length on this text in chapter 6, I want to highlight again God's purpose in discipline as revealed in this text. The writer of Hebrews reveals that discipline is designed to produce "holiness" (12:10) and "the peaceful fruit of righteousness" (12:11).

In verses 12 and 13 the writer emphasizes that discipline is intended to bring healing and restoration, because the Hebrew Christians were in danger of becoming disheartened and discouraged by the trials God was using in their lives. Reverting to the athletic imagery of 12:1–2, the writer insists that the Christians not be overwhelmed by weak hands and feeble knees—

injuries resulting from the disciplinary process. Rather, they must straighten out the course of their life "so that the limb which is lame may not be put out of joint, but rather be healed." God's discipline is not intended to permanently disable those who have been crippled by sin. Rather, His loving discipline is designed to restore and heal.

To Restore to a Former Condition—Gal. 6:1–2

While God's will for believers is that they be sanctified—set apart to God—and conformed increasingly to the image of Christ (1 Thess. 4:3; Rom. 6:12, 13; Col. 3:10), Paul acknowledges in Gal. 6:1 that Christians may occasionally sin (see also 1 John 2:1). Paul writes to the Galatian churches, "Brethren, even if a man is caught in any trespass, you who are spiritual, restore such a one in a spirit of gentleness; looking to yourself, lest you too be tempted."

The trespass

Paul visualizes a situation in which a believer is literally "overtaken" in or by a trespass. There is some debate as to whether the Christian is surprised *in* the midst of the transgression (i.e., caught "red handed")[2] or overtaken and caught *by* the transgression (i.e., ensnared by the deceitfulness of sin).[3] The Greek preposition *en* (translated "in" by the NASB) can have a locative (in, on, within, among) or instrumental (with, by means of) meaning. Lenski suggests that Paul is excluding willful, deliberate sin and referring to those transgressions which rise from ignorance, weakness, the deceptive power of sin, and the persuasion and example of others.[4] The last phrase, "lest you too be tempted," appears to suggest that Paul has in mind a kind of situation which may endanger even the most spiritual person.[5] Thus the context

---

[2]J.B. Lightfoot, *The Epistle of St. Paul to the Galatians* (Grand Rapids: Zondervan Publishing House, 1957), p. 215.

[3]James Montgomery Boice, "Galatians," in *The Expositor's Bible Commentary* vol. 10, ed. Frank E. Gaebelein (Grand Rapids: Zondervan Publishing House, 1976), p. 502.

[4]R.C.H. Lenski, *St. Paul's Epistles to the Galatians, Ephesians and Philippians* (Minneapolis: Augsburg Publishing House, 1961), p. 297.

[5]Homer Kent, Jr. objects to this view and offers the following comment: "Strictly speaking, one can be overtaken by temptation but not by transgression (*paraptomati*), for that requires an act of the individual." *The Freedom of God's Sons* (Grand Rapids: Baker Book House, 1976), p. 168.

points toward the "overtaken by the transgression" viewpoint.[6]

The word "transgression" literally means "to fall beside" and suggests the idea of falling along the way. As one who enjoys mountain climbing, I know the importance of carefully watching my steps when scaling a high peak. One false step or careless move can result in a disastrous fall. In the context of Gal. 6:1, "transgression" refers to an ethical violation or moral blunder. It is a sin which constitutes a departure from God's straight and narrow way.

What is to be done when we discover a Christian brother or sister has been ensnared by the clutches of sin? Usually we express shock ("I can't believe that Joe would do something like that!") and perhaps dismay ("What is the church coming to?"), and then we tell someone about it ("Say, did you hear what happened to. . ."). Such expressions of shock and dismay and gossip are often made under the guise of spirituality and concern ("I'm telling you this so you can pray for. . ."). Is this the way Paul would have us respond to a brother or sister who becomes entangled in sin?

Paul writes to the Galatians, "You who are spiritual, restore such a one . . ." Notice that Paul calls to action the "spiritual" Christians—those who are walking by the control of the Spirit and manifesting the fruits of the Spirit (Gal. 5:16, 22–24). Warren Wiersbe, former pastor of Moody Memorial Church, offers this probing thought: "The way you and I respond to someone who sins indicates whether or not we are spiritual."[7] Paul seems to be emphasizing that not all Christians, but Christians who are spiritually mature, should deal with sin in the lives of others. Not all may be qualified. Those who are weak, easily tempted, or unable to forgive should pray for the sinner (1 John 5:16), but leave the task of correction to others.

The restoration

The "spiritual" have the responsibility to restore the Christian who has fallen into sin. This concept of restoration is the key to

---

[6]In taking this position, we do not, however, deny there is a way of escape from every temptation (1 Cor. 10:13). Nor do we deny that man is totally responsible for his sinful actions (Acts 2:23).

[7]Warren Wiersbe, "When My Brother Sins," *Moody Monthly* (February 1983), p. 95.

this passage from Galatians, and is also the foundation stone of this book.

Consider restoration in light of your attitude toward your car. If your auto loses traction in snow or rain and slips off the road into the ditch, what do you do? Abandon it? Leave it to rust or be stripped by vandals? Of course not! You call the towing company to pull the car out of the ditch and transport it to the repair shop. There workmen beat out the dents, repair the engine, realign the wheels and restore the vehicle to good running order. That is God's attitude toward a fallen saint.

On May 8, 1981, mountaineers Jim Wickwire and Chris Kerrebrock were climbing Alaska's Mount McKinley when they both fell into a deep crevasse. Chris fell into the crevasse first, pulling a sled loaded with supplies on top of himself. Jim landed on top of the sled. After about 45 minutes of delicate climbing, Jim worked his way out of the crevasse. But his climbing partner was pinned facedown "like a piece of wood in a vise" in the 40-foot-deep crevasse. Although Jim attached a rope to Kerrebrock and tried to pull him out, he was unable to free the fallen climber.

Chris began suffering from hypothermia as night approached. Jim, exhausted from his attempts to free his friend, climbed out of the crevasse for the last time about 9 p.m. He was in shock and emotionally shattered. Chris probably died sometime early the next morning. Jim stayed at the site for eight days, however, until lack of food forced him to leave the mountain. He had done his best, but was unable to extract the fallen mountaineer from the grip of the crevasse.[8]

How often in the church we leave fallen Christians in the crevasse of sin without even taking the effort to restore them from their moral blunder. Certainly not all will be restored. Some might be so ensnared by sin that they are unwilling to repent and turn again to Christ. Some may resist the church's best efforts to return them to the straight and narrow way. But may we as Christians not be guilty of *abandoning* a believer in the crevasse of sin when all he or she needs is a little help to get out!

God makes a significant investment in the lives of His saints. Peter writes that Christians are "not redeemed with perishible things like silver and gold . . . but with precious blood as of a lamb unblemished and spotless, the blood of Christ" (1 Pet. 1:18–19). Paul calls the believer Christ's "inheritance" (Eph. 1:18). God

---

[8] *Oregon Journal* (May 15, 1981).

has an investment in the life of each believer. And it is encouraging to know that He never makes a bad investment! The concept of God's investment in the life of each believer should motivate every believer to share in the process of restoration.

The meaning of restoration

Mature Christians are to restore the person who has fallen into sin. What does the word "restore" mean? In classical Greek the verb *katartizo* had a wide variety of meanings which can be gathered under one of two headings: (1) "to adjust, to put in order, to restore"; (2) "to equip or fully furnish someone or something for a given purpose."[9] In the New Testament the word is used thirteen times, twice in quotations from the Old Testament (Matt. 21:16; Heb. 10:5). The basic meaning of the word is to "restore to its former condition."

Katartizo is used in Matt. 4:21 and Mark 1:19 with reference to James and John "mending" their torn or tangled fishing nets. During a summer sabbatical in 1983, I was privileged to visit Japan. Our family stayed several days in a Japanese inn at Katsura, a little fishing village on the Chiba peninsula. My children and I enjoyed watching the fishing boats unload their catches at the end of the day. The fish were placed in crates, covered with ice and then trucked to market. Near the area where the fish were being sorted and boxed sat a group of Japanese women with large spools of nylon cord, repairing fishing nets. The fishermen had made a sizable investment in the nets and could not afford to cast off such expensive equipment simply because of a tear. Careful, nimble fingers were busily restoring the damaged nets to their former condition.

Katartizo is used in Luke 6:40 in the sense of equipping someone for a purpose. There Jesus declares that a disciple will not be better-equipped than his teacher. In secular Greek the word is used of outfitting a ship for a voyage. In a military context it is used of an army, fully armed, equipped and prepared for battle. A ship sailing the Mediterranean without spare masts, sails, and ropes would be unthinkable (cf. Acts 27:19). A soldier entering battle without his sword, shield and helmet would be insane (cf. Eph. 6:13). As the disciple must be equipped for min-

---

[9]William Barclay, *New Testament Words* (London: SCM Press, Ltd., 1964), pp. 168–69.

istry, the ship for a voyage and the soldier for battle, so must a fallen Christian be reoutfitted, trained and equipped for dealing with the temptations he or she will certainly face.

Katartizo is used by secular Greek writers to denote joining together, or setting, a fractured or dislocated bone. When my brother broke his arm, the physician didn't just send him home with some pain pills. Neither did he amputate the injured limb. Instead, he carefully set the bone in the proper position and put the arm in a cast to immobilize it while the fracture mended. In the same vein, Paul may be employing the concept of "joining together" when he encourages the Corinthians to make an adjustment (*katartizo*) so that divisions and factions be avoided in the church (1 Cor. 1:10).

What implications does the meaning of *katartizo* have for our study of church discipline? First, the discipline of a saint is not designed to punish or destroy but rather to "mend" and "repair" someone who has been injured or damaged on the battlefield of life. Second, restoration involves equipping the saint with the spiritual principles necessary to avoid further injury and to meet the demands of the Christian life. Third, restoration is not simply the expression of forgiveness toward the sinner, but is a process of restoring the sinner to his former condition. The present tense of the verb *katartizo* in Gal. 6:1 suggests the necessity for patience and perseverance in the process of restoration.[10]

Drawing on the rich background of *katartizo*, Warren Wiersbe presents a challenging thought:

> When a brother or sister sins, the first response of the spiritually minded believer is to restore him or her. He says, "I want this part of the body to be strong and healthy. I want this net to be catching fish. I want this soldier to be fighting. I want this ship to be carrying cargo."[11]

Does this attitude match our way of dealing with those who sin? Often we inwardly rejoice when another Christian stumbles, thinking that the exposure of someone else's sin will make us look better. Or we broadcast the fallen Christian's failure throughout the Christian community, making restoration much more difficult. Or we turn aside and either neglect or reject the brother or sister who sins. Paul says, "No, Christian! Don't shoot

---

[10]W.E. Vine, *An Expository Dictionary of New Testament Words*, vol. 3 (Old Tappan, N.J.: Fleming H. Revell Company, 1940), p. 290.
[11]Wiersbe, "When My Brother Sins," p. 96.

that wounded soldier! Give him first aid and equip him to reenter the conflict!"

The manner of restoration

Paul offers two guidelines in Gal. 6:1 for those spiritual persons who would go to the aid of a wounded Christian. First, Paul says that the restoration ought to be done "in a spirit of gentleness." The word "gentleness" (NASB) or "meekness" (KJV) is the same word (*prautes*) used in the list of Spirit-produced virtues in Gal. 5:22. While our English word "meekness" is often equated with weakness, the Greek word *prautes* has no such implication. It does not suggest weakness, hesitation or compromise. In classical Greek the verb form of the word was used to speak of taming wild animals. Hence, the word implies strength under control.

For the Christian, *prautes* is a condition of the heart and mind which evokes courteous, considerate, thoughtful and humble dealings with others. It is the opposite of pride, self-assertiveness and self-interest. The meek, or gentle, Christian is neither shocked nor dismayed at the failure of others, for he is not occupied with making comparisons.

Church discipline, says Paul, is to be carried out in an atmosphere of gentleness. The gentle person God uses to help restore a sinning saint will be firm and uncompromising, and will never deny the awfulness of sin. But the person God uses will also show Christlike consideration for the fallen believer. The words of the hymn writer, Kate B. Wilkinson, express well both the source and result of the virtue of gentleness: "May the mind of Christ my Savior live in me from day to day, by His love and power controlling all I do and say."

Paul's second guideline for those helping in the restoration process is that they beware lest they too fall into temptation. Paul warns, "Restore such a one in a spirit of gentleness, looking to yourself, lest you too be tempted." The word "looking" means more than just seeing the facts. It implies mental consideration. The Greek word (*skopeo*) is the one from which we derive our words "microscope" and "telescope." It suggests the idea of looking with contemplation and reflection.

Paul indicates that paying close attention to ourselves—our attitudes and actions—is for the purpose of avoiding a careless response to seductive temptation. But are we not talking about the "spiritual" Christian? Certainly those who have the spiritual maturity, insight and ability to restore a fallen sinner would not succumb to the same sin! "Don't count on it," says Paul. He is warning the spiritual Christian to beware of the deceitfulness of sin, not to let it catch us by surprise or take us unaware. In the process of correcting and restoring others, we must watch our steps, lest we too succumb to Satan's schemes!

Even the most mature can be duped. On the night of December 6, 1942, Admiral Kimmel, Commander in Chief of the Pacific Fleet, attended a dinner party with a number of important naval commanders and their wives. One woman there, the wife of Admiral Halsey, insisted the Japanese were going to attack. But everyone at the dinner party thought she was crazy. Twelve hours later the Japanese bombed Pearl Harbor, destroying most of the U.S. Navy's Pacific Fleet.

At a naval inquiry in 1944, Admiral Leary spoke of the complacency at the dinner and at the daily conferences held by Admiral Kimmel during the weeks preceding the attack. When asked whether any thought had been given to the possibility of a surprise attack by the Japanese, he said, "We all felt that the contingency was remote. . . ." The same attitude was expressed by other naval officers: "We always felt that it couldn't happen here." Admiral Kimmel's advisors concurred that they acted on the basis of an "unwarranted feeling of immunity from attack." Their lack of vigilance led them down the pathway to unexpected disaster.

Paul is warning all Christians who would come to the aid of a wounded soldier, "Don't operate under the delusion that you are immune to attack." A.T. Robertson, the noted Greek grammarian, offers this warning: "Spiritual experts (preachers in particular) need this caution. Satan loves a shining mark."[12]

Being burden-bearers

Paul adds a further note on Gal. 6:2 to encourage mature Christians to share in the work of restoring a sinning saint. He says, "Bear one another's burdens, and thus fulfill the law of Christ."[13] While this verse has been applied (and rightly so) to

---

[12]A.T. Robertson, *Word Pictures in the New Testament*, vol. 2: *The Epistles of Paul* (Nashville: Broadman Press, 1931), p. 315.

[13]There is no contradiction between Gal. 6:2 and 6:5. It is the duty of every Christian to carry his own "pack" or load (6:5), but those who have a burden more heavy than they can bear should be given assistance (6:2).

many different situations in which Christian love may be expressed, the application in this context concerns church discipline. Believers ought to be concerned about helping other Christians recover from moral lapses. The Galatians are exhorted to "keep on bearing one another's burdens."

What burdens might Paul have in mind? Perhaps the burdens may be thoughts of the shame, grief, depression, and remorse that result from the exposure of one's sin. Perhaps they are the discipline, the loss of position, and the difficult circumstances experienced by the Christian who has undergone moral catastrophe. Whatever the burden, Paul exhorts the believers not to let the brother or sister bear it alone. Others need to come alongside and give help when it is needed.

The motivation for such aid is none other than Christ's law of love. The "law of Christ" refers to the principle of love for God and for one another (Deut. 6:5; Lev. 19:18; John 13:34, 35), which serves as the basis for God's instructions in both the law and the prophets (Matt. 22:34–40).

It appears quite clear from our study of Gal. 6:1–2 and other related texts that God designed church discipline to restore fallen saints. That objective ought to be preeminent in any disciplinary action within the church, for sharing in the recovery of one of God's flock is a precious privilege—and a weighty responsibility. Discipline must be done firmly, yet gently, and always out of love. Those who share in the process also share in the joy of seeing a saint restored. Does not the Father rejoice over the recovery of the one sheep more than over the ninety-nine which have not gone astray (Matt. 18:13)?

8
RESTORATION AFTER DISCIPLINE

Donna was an elder's wife at an independent Bible church. She served actively as a Sunday school teacher in the Junior department and was an officer in the Women's Missionary Fellowship. Her husband was shocked when he discovered she was involved in an affair with another man—a professing Christian.

Donna's husband, Stan, was overwhelmed by the realization of his wife's unfaithfulness. He brought the matter to the church's pastor. Donna was then approached by the pastoral staff who urged her to repent. After several weeks and no indication of repentance, Donna's affair was brought to the attention of the board of elders. At this point Donna began to show a change of heart. She stopped seeing the other man and confessed her sin to her husband. At the request of the elder board, she resigned from her Sunday school teaching and her office in the Women's Missionary Fellowship. She eventually met with the pastoral staff and her life bears the signs of genuine repentance.

Although the board decided to keep Donna's sin a private matter, somehow her affair became known. Rumors circulated for several months, but then quieted down. It has been five years since Donna repented of her unfaithfulness. She has not repeated her sin. But she has never again been asked to serve as a Sunday school teacher. Sensing a lack of acceptance by the ladies in the Missionary Fellowship, Donna no longer attends their meetings. God has forgiven Donna's sin, but since her affair, she has not experienced close fellowship with the church family she once loved and served. Both Donna and her husband Stan are on the brink of bitterness and resentment.

Ralph, a single man, was a church leader and an active discipler, a faithful attender at the weekly men's prayer breakfast and a lover of theological discussion. His life, from all appearances, was above reproach. Therefore the pastor was quite surprised when he read in the Saturday paper that Ralph had been arrested for propositioning a police "decoy."

The pastor and a church elder visited Ralph in jail. At that time Ralph insisted he had only "wanted to talk to" the woman; he hadn't intended to have sexual relations with her. He neither acknowledged nor confessed any real sin. After Ralph's release the matter of his conduct was brought before the church board. Ralph's roommate revealed that Ralph's arrest was not a one-time occurrence. Ralph had been involved in numerous incidents of immorality.

The steps of Matt. 18:15–17 were carefully followed, giving ample time for repentance and change after each stage. When the matter was lovingly and grievingly shared with the congregation, the brother left the church rather than confess and repent of his wrong.

Five years passed. During that time God worked on Ralph's heart. After five years of heartache, misery and resisting God, Ralph wrote a letter of confession and repentance which was read to the church. The church board then met with him and discerned that his repentance was genuine. Rejoicing, they literally gave him a new sport coat, had a gold ring made for his finger, and celebrated with him over a veal dinner! Ralph has walked with God ever since.

Discipline is a high priority and heavy responsibility of Christ's church. Restoration is its ultimate aim. When a sin is confessed and genuine repentance is evidenced, how ought the church family to respond? I am afraid that the tendency is to hold a repentant sinner at arm's length. We think we can't trust him anymore. Somehow his life is tainted. Full restoration to joyful fellowship with the church family, therefore, is frequently, and inadvertently, denied. What kind of follow-up is necessary after church discipline that leads to genuine repentance?

The Steps for Full Restoration—2 Cor. 2:5–9

In 1 Corinthians 5, Paul directs the Corinthian believers to discipline a brother who is sexually involved with his stepmother. Paul rebukes the church for its prideful attitude and absence of grief over this sin. He also warns the church that a "little leaven leavens the whole lump." His final words on this point are, "Remove the wicked man from yourselves" (1 Cor. 5:13). And the church did. The unrepentant sinner was excommunicated from the assembly.

When Paul writes 2 Corinthians, about eight months have passed since he had ordered the removal of the sinner from the Corinthian church. What has resulted from this firm discipline? Praise the Lord, the sinner has repented! But the Corinthian church has failed to acknowledge such repentance and to follow up with loving affirmation of the repentant sinner.[1]

The sorrowful steps of discipline carried out by the Corinthian church at Paul's direction have accomplished their purpose. Genuine repentance has taken place. For this reason Paul can say the punishment has proved "sufficient" (2:6). The discipline has accomplished its purpose. It is now the duty of the disciplining body to encourage reconciliation and restoration to fellowship. The important place of such follow-up is stressed by P. E. Hughes:

> Discipline which is so inflexible as to leave no place for repentance and reconciliation has ceased to be truly Christian; for it is no less a scandal to cut off the penitent sinner from all hope of re-entry into the comfort and security of the fellowship of the redeemed community than it is to permit flagrant wickedness to continue unpunished in the body of Christ.[2]

Notice that the discipline was not the decision or prerogative of just one person. The discipline was carried out "by the majority" (2:6). We are not told whether a formal meeting of the church was convened, and whether the decision was by vote or general consensus.[3] In some way, however, the "whole group" or "main body" (*hoi pleiones*) was involved in administering the dis-

---

[1]Until recently, it was practically the universal conclusion of the church that the incident of incest in 1 Corinthians 5 provides the background for Paul's words in 2 Cor. 2:5–11. Some have maintained, however, that Paul could not have so readily encouraged the restoration of one guilty of such sin. But Paul's purpose in ordering the discipline was remedial—"that his spirit may be saved" (1 Cor. 5:5). With P. E. Hughes, I believe there is no compelling reason to abandon the view that Paul in 2 Corinthians 2 is following up on the 1 Corinthians 5 incident. *Commentary on the Second Epistle to the Corinthians* (Grand Rapids: Wm. B. Eerdmans Publishing Co., 1962), pp. 59–65.

[2]Hughes, *Commentary on the Second Epistle to the Corinthians*, pp. 66–67.

[3]Murray J. Harris, "Second Corinthians," in *The Expositor's Bible Commentary* vol. 10, ed. Frank E. Gaebelein (Grand Rapids: Zondervan Publishing House, 1976), p. 329.

cipline. In obedience to the Apostle's instructions, the church family had joined together in the disciplinary process. Now Paul exhorts the Corinthians to join together in the vital matter of disciplinary follow-up.

Forgive him

The Corinthians had effectively administered the discipline Paul had ordered. They were failing, however, to match the offender's repentance with their forgiveness.[4] Paul insists that, in view of the sinner's repentance, the church's role must change—"so that on the contrary you should rather forgive. . ." (2:7).

According to Jesus there is but one condition for forgiveness: repentance. "If your brother sins, rebuke him, and if he repents, forgive him" (Luke 17:3). The word "repents" translates the Greek word *metanoew*, which literally means "to change the mind." The one who has repented has changed his mind about sin, agreeing with God that it is evil. But more than a change of mind is implied. The concept of repentance is illustrated in 1 Thessalonians 1:9 where Paul writes of the Thessalonians who "turned to God from idols to serve a living and true God." Repentance means a change in *actions* resulting from a change in *convictions*. It suggests a 180-degree "about face" with regard to sin.

The question is frequently asked by those seeking to administer church discipline, "How do we know that the repentance is genuine?" John the Baptist told the multitudes to "bring forth fruits in keeping with your repentance" (Luke 3:8). Paul told the Gentiles "they should repent and turn to God, performing deeds appropriate to repentance" (Acts 26:20). It appears, therefore, that genuine repentance will make itself evident by its deeds. The truly repentant sinner will freely acknowledge his sin (1 John 1:9). The truly repentant sinner will seek to make restitution for the wrong done, especially if material loss or property damage has resulted (Philem. 18–19). The truly repentant person will exhibit genuine sorrow over sin (2 Cor. 7:8–10). The truly repentant person will manifest the fruit of the Spirit: "love, joy, peace, patience, kindness, goodness, faithfulness, gentleness, self-control" (Gal. 5:22–23).

Of course a skilled hypocrite may display such outward manifestations without any inward change. But while he may fool

---

[4]Robert B. Hughes, *Second Corinthians* (Chicago: Moody Press, 1983), p. 36.

other believers, God knows the heart. He is not fooled by deeds of "righteousness" which don't issue from the heart. And God-given discernment may enable church leaders to identify such sham.

There is one danger in looking for the "fruits of repentance": the tendency to respond judgmentally, saying such things as, "There is not enough. It hasn't been long enough. He is just sorry he got caught. I'm not ready yet to forgive." If a brother or sister confesses sin (agreeing with God that it is wrong), turns from sin, and seeks restoration, we have no right to withhold forgiveness from that person. It is better to forgive and occasionally err on the side of grace than to withhold forgiveness from one who might genuinely deserve it.

What does forgiveness mean? There are two words used in the New Testament to signify forgiveness. In 2 Cor. 2:7 Paul uses *charizomai* which is based on the root "grace." This word emphasizes that forgiveness is an unconditional gift, the result of favor, not earned by works of merit. The word used most frequently in the New Testament for forgiveness is *aphiemi*, literally translated "to send forth" or "to send away." The word implies the remission of a debt—the debt of sin (Matt. 6:12). Forgiveness may be defined as the gracious act of no longer holding a person accountable for his sin. Genuine forgiveness means that the sin will never be brought up again. As much as is possible from a human perspective, the matter is to be forgotten. God himself said of His repentant people, "I will forgive their iniquity, and their sin I will remember no more" (Jer. 31:34; cf. Isa. 43:25).

A friend of Clara Barton, founder of the American Red Cross, once reminded her of an especially cruel thing that had been done to Clara years before. But Miss Barton seemed not to recall it. "Don't you remember it?" her friend insisted. "No," came the reply, "I distinctly remember forgetting it." That is true forgiveness.

Forgiveness may be illustrated by what happens when I am balancing my checkbook and suddenly push the wrong button on my calculator. In a flash all the data I have put into the device is eliminated. There is no record of the previous information. I must start my calculations again with a "blank sheet." That is what happens when God forgives. And His actions provide a model for forgiveness on a human level.

But what if the repentant sinner falls back into sin? How many times should we be willing to forgive? Shouldn't there be a limit? Peter thought so, and asked, "Lord, how often shall my brother sin against me and I forgive him? Up to seven times?" (Matt. 18:21). Peter knew the Pharisees said that three times was enough. He doubled that figure and added one for good measure. Certainly seven times would be enough. To offer more forgiveness would make a mockery of grace and encourage sin!

The Lord's response to Peter was a challenge to the disciple's faith. "I do not say to you, up to seven times, but up to seventy times seven" (Matt. 18:22). In other words, Jesus was saying, "Genuine forgiveness knows no limit. It is a state of the heart (18:35), not a matter of mere mathematical calculation. Peter, if you are still counting, it is not enough."

Elsewhere Jesus says, "And if he sins against you seven times a day, and returns to you seven times, saying, 'I repent,' forgive him" (Luke 17:4). Even the apostles had difficulty with the concept of "unlimited" forgiveness. They replied, "Increase our faith!" (Luke 17:5). Leon Morris comments: "From the world's point of view a sevenfold repetition of an offense in one day must cast doubt on the genuineness of the sinner's repentance. But that is not the believer's concern. His business is forgiveness."[5]

A pastor inadvertently offended a church member by the manner in which he handled some church business. When this came to the pastor's attention, he sought out the person and apologized. Several months later the pastor discovered that the offended saint was still holding a grudge—he wouldn't believe the pastor's apology was "sincere."

What must a person do to communicate the sincerity of an apology? Flagellate himself and then come crawling on broken glass? The Christian's responsibility is to match loving forgiveness with the sinner's confession and repentance. Only God can ultimately judge the verity of such actions.

Forgiveness should be *communicated* to the repentant offender. We should never minimize the issue and say, "Well, it's all right. Let's just forget it." Rather, we should say something like, "I recognize you've committed a sin and I appreciate your expression of repentance. I do forgive you." In one church, following the confession and repentance of an immoral member, the pastor invited all those who wished to communicate their

---

[5]Leon Morris, *The Gospel According to St. Luke* (Grand Rapids: Wm. B. Eerdmans Publishing Co., 1974), p. 256.

forgiveness to the repentant sister to stand. To the pastor's surprise, the whole congregation rose from the pews. It was a tangible expression of forgiveness by the church, and a sweet restoration for the repentant sinner.

Comfort him

Not only should the church family forgive the sinning saint, but it should, as Paul commands, "comfort him." The word translated "comfort" is the Greek word *parakaleo*, which literally means "to call alongside." In first-century Greek literature the word denotes summoning aid or invoking help. In military contexts the word speaks of the encouragement of soldiers who are in the heat of battle. In the noun form, the word is used of those who are "called alongside to help"—military reinforcements. In many New Testament contexts, *parakaleo* is translated "encourage, comfort, exhort, urge."

Paul is saying that the believers need to "come alongside" a disciplined saint so that he may be comforted, encouraged and exhorted to go on in the faith. The necessity of this kind of a ministry is reflected by the last clause in 2 Cor. 2:7 "lest somehow such a one be overwhelmed by excessive sorrow." Paul knows that church discipline can be very painful; in 2 Cor. 7:8–10 he associates "sorrow" with the discipline which leads to repentance.

A godly sorrow can be very therapeutic, purging the soul to ready it for repentance. But eventually sorrow must cease. To perpetuate it may result in discouragement, despair and even depression. Paul is warning the Corinthians that they should come alongside a repentant sinner so that he will not be overwhelmed, literally "swallowed up," by excessive sorrow. R.V.G. Tasker comments, ". . . if such sorrow lasts too long or is felt too acutely, it may have a crushing rather than a remedial effect, and perhaps drive the victim into isolation and despair."[6]

Many sincere Christians, tragically, fail in this important responsibility of coming alongside a brother or sister who has fallen into sin. Repentance has taken place and forgiveness has been granted. But then the matter is forgotten. Busy Christians go on their way and about their ministries while the wounded soldier is still suffering from "battle fatigue." His world has been shat-

---

[6]R.V.G. Tasker, *The Second Epistle of Paul to the Corinthians* (Grand Rapids: Wm. B. Eerdmans Publishing Co., 1958), p. 54.

tered by the exposure of his sin and the trauma of his public confession. Where are the saints who should help bear this brother's burden?

Some are just busy and forgetful. They care, but lack sensitivity and empathy toward those in need. Others are genuinely concerned, but feel uncomfortable and self-conscious initiating a personal contact—in the same way they feel uncomfortable speaking with someone who has recently lost a loved one. Should they mention the recent tragedy or just ignore it? Such people have yet to realize that their presence, not consoling words, will best communicate loving concern. By reaching out to a hurting brother or sister, we say, "I care about you. Your failure has not jeopardized our relationship. You will always be my friend."

Still others do not reach out to a repentant sinner because they either are unwilling to fully forgive or are unsure if the repentance is genuine. They withhold full restoration to fellowship until sufficient time has passed to ensure the sinner has mastered the temptation and experienced complete victory over sin. But is this consistent with true forgiveness and Christlike love? A repentant sinner needs immediate help and encouragement. That is why Paul admonishes the Corinthians to come alongside and encourage the brother who has repented from his sin.

Love him

In 2 Cor. 2:8 Paul declares, "Wherefore [the strongest Greek word for stating a conclusion] I urge you to reaffirm love for him." Hughes comments, "Repentance must be met by full restoration in love."[7] The word translated "reaffirm" is commonly used in legal documents of the first century in connection with their ratification. Ratification demonstrated the validity or binding nature of a document (cf. Gal. 3:15). Paul is therefore encouraging the Corinthians to demonstrate the reality and commitment of their love for the repentant brother. It was not enough for the Corinthians to say, "We love you." Paul wants them to give tangible proof of this love in their restoration of the repentant sinner.

The *agape* love of which Paul speaks is not a mere feeling or affection. This love is from God (1 John 4:7). It is produced in

---

[7]R.B. Hughes, *Second Corinthians*, p. 36.

the life of the believer by the Holy Spirit (Gal. 5:22). Jesus identified this *agape* as the mark of the Christian (John 13:34, 35). It
is the love of John 3:16, of sacrifice and commitment. This love
is to be the very essence of the Christian's love. Paul says, "Keep
on walking in love" (Eph. 5:2); "Let all you do be done in love"
(1 Cor. 16:14); "Abound in love for one another" (1 Thess. 3:12).
This *agape* love is a sacrificial commitment produced in the heart
of the Christian by the Holy Spirit, and energized by a deliberate
conviction that wills the very best for others.

Paul expects the Corinthians to overcome any negative feelings they may have and give *tangible* evidence of their commitment to the ultimate good of the repentant sinner. This kind of
love can be expressed personally by a card or letter, or congre-
gationally by a plant or bouquet of flowers. A faculty member at
a Christian school had to resign due to the exposure of a personal
sin. After his confession and tearful repentance, the faculty
members showed their love toward the former colleague by starting a fund to provide him with money until he could secure
another position. Such actions do more than say, "We love you."
They give tangible evidence of the Christians' commitment to
the ultimate good of a repentant sinner.

The Danger of an Unforgiving Spirit

Someone once told John Wesley, "I never forgive." Wesley
wisely replied, "Then sir, I hope that you never sin." Those who
are unwilling to forgive others put themselves in great jeopardy.
Both Paul and Jesus warn of the dangers of an unforgiving spirit.

The schemes of Satan—2 Cor. 2:9–11

Paul tells the Corinthians that their response to his instructions regarding the repentant sinner had been a "test" determin-
ing whether they were "obedient in all things" (2:9). To forgive,
comfort, and reaffirm love would prove obedience to the Apostle's instructions. Failure to follow up on the matter of church
discipline would involve a serious breach of Paul's commands.
He sets the example for forgiveness in verse 10 by informing the
Corinthians that he has already forgiven the repentant sinner.
The words, "if I have forgiven anything," certainly reflect Paul's
view that the sin of 1 Corinthians 5 was primarily "an offence

against the church within which it was committed."[8] That the sin was forgiven "in the presence of Christ" suggests that Paul did so with Christ's authority and approval (cf. Matt. 18:18–35).

In verse 11 Paul further explains what he meant by "for your sakes" in verse 10: "In order that no advantage be taken of us by Satan; for we are not ignorant of his schemes." If the repentant sinner is not forgiven and restored to fellowship, Satan will use the situation to advance his purposes. Failure to encourage full restoration after repentance is to play into the hands of Satan who is already causing discord and dissension in the Corinthian church (1 Cor. 1:11,12). The words "no advantage be taken" translate the Greek word "to have more," which suggests "having more than one's due." Failure to restore the repentant sinner will give Satan more claim on the church than he is due. It will give him an advantage that he certainly doesn't deserve.

Paul explains his concern in the last phrase: "for we are not ignorant of his schemes." Satan has many evil plans and purposes—plots for moral disaster and spiritual deadness which he would love to unleash on the church. Since the Corinthians are fully aware of Satan's wicked designs, they ought to forgive, comfort, and reaffirm love for the sinning brother. Failure to do so is to give a victory to Satan. It would be like Roy Riegels' history-making touchdown in the 1929 Rose Bowl—he scored for the opposing team!

The absence of blessing—Matt. 6:14, 15

In His Sermon on the Mount, Jesus teaches that the forgiveness we receive is in proportion to the forgiveness we give. "For if you forgive men for their transgressions, your heavenly Father will also forgive you" (Matt. 6:14). Jesus then reveals a sobering truth: Our refusal to forgive others means that our forgiveness is in jeopardy. "If you do not forgive men, then your Father will not forgive your transgressions" (Matt. 6:15).

Jesus is not suggesting, of course, that our salvation rests on good works rather than the grace and mercy of God (cf. Luke 18:13; Eph. 2:8; Titus 3:5). Fellowship with God, therefore, and not salvation from sin, seems to be the subject of this text. Jesus is saying that one of the plain indicators of our relationship to Christ is our willingness to forgive others. Louis Barbieri ex-

---

[8]P.E. Hughes, *Commentary on the Second Epistle to the Corinthians*, p. 70.

plains, "One cannot walk in fellowship with God if he refuses to forgive others."[9]

Those who acknowledge their own sins and fully forgive others are those who are rightly related to Christ and enjoy His blessing. Jesus is simply saying that God will not bless an unforgiving heart. This passage challenges us to be gracious and forgiving toward those who have sinned. Our response to a repentant sinner should reflect where we are in our relationship with Christ. And, as Paul points out, forgiveness ought to be reciprocal ("forgiving each other"), reflecting the fact that "God in Christ also has forgiven you" (Eph. 4:32).

The forfeiture of mercy—Matt. 18:21–35

After instructing Peter that genuine forgiveness knows no limitation (Matt. 18:21, 22), Jesus presents a parable which illustrates the nature of forgiveness in Christ's kingdom (Matt. 18:23–35). Jesus tells of a king's servant who incurred an enormous debt that was about to result in his being sold into slavery, along with his wife and children. But out of compassion and mercy, the king forgave the debt. Then the servant proceeded to threaten and imprison a fellow slave who owed him a mere pittance. When the king learned of the unforgiving servant's actions, he summoned him and said, "Should you not also have had mercy on your fellow-slave, even as I had mercy on you?" (v. 33). Then the king retracted his forgiveness and forced the payment of the debt.

Jesus makes a pointed application of the parable in Matthew: "So shall My heavenly Father also do to you, if each of you does not forgive his brother from your heart" (v. 35). There is a great lesson here for the Christian church. In view of the debt forgiven us (Rom. 5:8; 1 Cor. 6:9–11), no injustice is too great for a believer to forgive one who requests forgiveness. Refusal to do so may jeopardize God's merciful dealings with us.

The Example of Restoration—Luke 15:11–32

In Luke 15 Jesus uses three parables to show His disciples God's attitude toward sinners. Believing that God hates sinners, the Pharisees were refusing any association with those who failed

---

[9]Louis A. Barbieri, Jr., "Matthew," in *The Bible Knowledge Commentary*, eds. J.F. Walvoord and R.B. Zuck (Wheaton: Victor Books, 1983), p. 32.

to keep the law. Jesus uses the parables to show that sinners are the special objects of God's affection! God actively seeks sinners to bring them to himself, and He exults with great joy when a lost sinner is found.

The parable of the Prodigal (i.e., "addicted to wasteful expenditure") Son (Luke 15:11–32) may be well-called the parable of the Searching Father, for he is mentioned eight times. We are all familiar with this beloved story. Taking his inheritance, the younger of the two sons squandered his wealth through wild living. Having lost all, he sank to the pit of degradation—feeding swine and feeling hungry enough to eat their food. Then the son came to his senses and returned home, hoping to join the ranks of his father's hired men.

While the young man was still a long way down the road, the compassionate and forgiving father saw him coming and ran to greet him. The prodigal son confessed, "Father, I have sinned against heaven and in your sight; I am no longer worthy to be called your son" (Luke 15:21). To the youth's surprise the father adorned his repentant son with his best robe, put a ring on his finger and sandals on his feet. He ordered the fattened calf to be prepared for a great feast, explaining, "For this son of mine was dead, and has come to life again; he was lost, and has been found. And they began to make merry" (Luke 15:24).

The loving father fully forgave and restored the repentant son to blessed fellowship. He didn't refuse to forgive or require a waiting period to make sure the repentance was genuine. He not only forgave the wayward son, but he encouraged him with gifts and expressions of love. The forgiving father stands in stark contrast to the older son who was angered by the compassionate gestures and the rejoicing over his brother's return.

Where do we stand in our attitude toward repentant sinners? Do we condemn them as the self-righteous son? Or do we forgive and restore them as the loving father?

9

THE RESULTS OF CHURCH DISCIPLINE

Tom was happily married and the father of two lovely children. He was a hard-working insurance salesman, enjoying a growing business. Because of the increase in clients to service, he set up an office and proceeded to hire a part-time secretary. One of the most likely prospects was a young woman Tom knew from the church choir. Janet, an attractive divorcee, was looking for a part-time job to supplement the income she received as a school food service worker.

Janet soon proved her effectiveness in the office, handling calls, organizing files, and relieving Tom of many business details. Being a warm and friendly person, Janet made Tom feel very comfortable with her in the office. They enjoyed each other's company and shared a few "business" lunches together. But before long, talk about the insurance business turned to more personal subjects. Tom began discussing matters with Janet which he should have been discussing with his wife. In the office, Tom would gently place his hand on Janet's shoulder while giving instructions. Before he knew what had happened, Tom and Janet were emotionally involved with each other. Although Tom still loved his wife, he sought more private times with Janet. Physical touching and intimate conversation, however, led to the inevitable—an "accident" occurred.

By this time Tom's wife, Carol, was suspecting her husband's intimate involvement with his secretary. She sought the counsel of her pastor, who then invited Bob out for lunch. In the course of the conversation, Tom admitted his affair with Janet and sought advice on how to avoid marital disaster. Tom was a reasonable man. He loved Carol and his children, and did not want them to suffer as a result of his infatuation with Janet. So the pastor asked him to meet with two of the church elders to decide the best course of action. Janet was also asked to attend the meeting.

Both Tom and Janet expressed genuine repentance. Their sin had, as they explained it, "taken them by surprise." Together, the pastor and elders, with Tom and Janet, decided Janet should immediately resign from being Tom's secretary. Because of the immorality involved, they also decided that both Tom and Janet should cease their participation in the church choir until their repentance had proven genuine and their affair had truly ended. Since both were repentant and the sin was not known to the church, the elders determined that it would not be necessary to make any public disclosure of the matter. In time, both were fully restored and rejoined the choir. There have been no further problems.

Things don't always turn out this well, but most people would consider this case of church discipline "successful." What are the results when church discipline succeeds? What happens when it fails?

When Discipline Succeeds

In Matt. 18:12–14 Jesus tells a familiar parable of the shepherd who leaves his ninety-nine sheep to search for the one which has gone astray. Following this parable, Jesus proceeds to discuss the steps of church discipline (Matt. 18:15–20). The parable serves to introduce the subject of church discipline and to illustrate the purpose that such discipline is to accomplish.

The parable of the lost sheep concludes with Jesus' comment about the attitude of the shepherd toward the recovery of the sheep: "And if it turns out that he finds it, truly I say to you, he rejoices over it more than over the ninety-nine which have not gone astray." Jesus acknowledges by the use of the conditional clause ("if") that the recovery of the lost sheep is a possibility, but not a certainty. Jesus also highlights the great rejoicing by the shepherd when the lost sheep is found.

Church discipline is designed to restore sinning saints. By God's grace, this is frequently its result. In addition to the restoration of the delinquent saint, there are some very significant extra benefits for the church which employs the disciplinary process.

Reaping the results—Acts 5:1–14

Acts 5 records the sin of Ananias and Sapphira and the resulting first divine judgment in the early church. Satan had been unable to thwart the message of the resurrection by attacking the church from without (Acts 4:19–20), so he attempted to undermine the purity of the church from within. This account is to Acts what the story of Achan is to Joshua. In both situations God was inaugurating a great work. He therefore severely judged the first appearance of sin in order to emphasize the vital need for purity among the people of God.

The sin of Ananias and Sapphira was not their keeping part of the proceeds from the sale of their property, but their pretending to give to the church *all* they had received. F. F. Bruce comments:

> Ananias, in the effort to gain a reputation for greater generosity than he actually deserved, tried to deceive the believing community, but in trying to deceive the community he was really trying to deceive the Holy Spirit, whose life-giving power had created the community and maintained it in being.[1]

Ananias and Sapphira played the part of religious hypocrites—pretending greater devotion than they actually had. This was, in essence, lying to the Holy Spirit (5:3). Ananias and Sapphira were putting God "to the test" (5:9). They were presuming upon His goodness and patience in dealing with sin.

Ananias and Sapphira may not have intended to "put the Spirit of the Lord to the test," but they did so just the same. Lenski observes:

> Sinners often call their sins by mild but untrue names. When the light of God falls upon them, all shams disappear. Every imitation of faith and of love tempts the Spirit, challenges him.[2]

The temptation to seek a greater reputation than is due us for our generosity, spiritual piety or some other virtue is not uncommon among Christians. Rather than adopting a self-righteous attitude toward Ananias and Sapphira, we might do well to take a warning from their example.

The Lord used Peter, not to call down divine judgment, but

---

[1] F.F. Bruce, *The Book of Acts* NIC NT (Grand Rapids: Wm. B. Eerdmans Publishing Co., 1954), p. 113.

[2] R.C.H. Lenski, *The Acts of the Apostles* (Minneapolis: Augsburg Publishing House, 1961), p. 204.

to point out the sin. "Ananias, why has Satan filled your heart to lie to the Holy Spirit, and to keep back some of the price of the land?" As Peter spoke the words, God judged Ananias with physical death. "And as he heard these words, Ananias fell down and breathed his last." Shortly thereafter, Sapphira, who had conspired with her husband in this deception, entered the house. Peter gave her the opportunity to tell the truth: "Tell me whether you sold the land for such and such a price?" Sapphira repeated her husband's lie and shared his fate.

Obviously, in this particular case, the deaths of Ananias and Sapphira were the result of divine judgment rather than church discipline. Nevertheless, the effects of this judgment on the believing community in Jerusalem are quite instructive. This account serves to illustrate some of the potential results of church discipline.

1. Renewed fear

The first result of this historic act of discipline in the early church is noted in verse 11: "And great fear came upon the whole church, and upon all who heard of these things" (cf. 5:5). The strong emphasis today on the *love* of God has frequently resulted in Christians neglecting the concept of the *fear* of God. The "fear of the Lord" is the first and most important step in one's pursuit of wisdom (Job. 28:28; Ps. 111:10; Prov. 9:10). It serves as the theme of Proverbs (1:7) and the conclusion of Ecclesiastes (12:13). The "fear of the Lord" characterizes the ideal woman (Prov. 31:30) and the successful man (Ps. 115:13). The fear of the Lord essentially is a reverential appreciation of God and recognition of our accountability before Him.

The wisdom writers give us a clue as to how the "fear of the Lord" is to be applied in the life of a believer. They link the fear of God with such actions as "departing from evil" and "obeying God's commandments" (Job. 28:28; Ps. 111:10). The one who sincerely "fears God" recognizes that he serves an awesome, holy God. The writer of Hebrews expresses a healthy "fear of God" when he writes, ". . . let us show gratitude, by which we may offer to God an acceptable service with reverence and awe; for our God is a consuming fire" (12:28b, 29).

Those who witnessed God's judgment on Ananias and Sapphira had a healthy concept of the "fear of God" rekindled within their hearts. Many a Christian in the Jerusalem church probably trembled and said, "But for the grace of God, there go I." Many undoubtedly renewed their commitment to live holy, God-honoring lives.

2. Unity enhanced

The second result of the judgment on Ananias and Sapphira was the enhancement of church unity. Luke records, "And at the hands of the apostles many signs and wonders were taking place among the people; and they were all with one accord in Solomon's portico" (Acts 5:12). The church was meeting together regularly in the long, roomy colonnaded porch along the east wall in the temple court at Jerusalem. They were "all" there and "with one accord."

Church unity must be a high priority for Christians. It is, after all, very important to Jesus. In His prayer for His future disciples, Jesus requests His Father "that they may all be one; even as Thou, Father, are in Me, and I in Thee. . . . And the glory which Thou hast given Me I have given to them; that they may be one, just as We are one; I in them, and Thou in Me, that they may be perfected in unity, that the world may know that Thou didst send Me" (John 17:21–23).

How is church unity attained? Church unity develops as we take time to make it a priority. Specifically, we must (1) recognize the common spiritual heritage believers share—cf. Eph. 4:3–6; (2) help believers who have a dispute to become reconciled to each other—Phil. 4:2, 3; (3) consider others as more important than ourselves—Phil. 2:3, 4; and (4) bear one another's burdens—Gal. 6:2. The Jerusalem church found its unity enhanced through careful and impartial congregational discipline. Church discipline that follows biblical guidelines will have similar results today.

3. Purity preserved

A third result of the judgment on Ananias and Sapphira was preservation of the church's purity. Luke writes, "But none of the rest dared to associate with them; however, the people held them in high esteem" (Acts 5:13). Not only had the divine discipline purged the church of a deceitful sin, but it caused others of questionable moral conduct, and perhaps less than genuine faith, to avoid identifying themselves with the Christian community.

Church discipline should result in a purified church. Paul ordered the Corinthian church to exercise church discipline on the brother who was involved in an immoral relationship, and he used a metaphor of purification: "Clean out the old leaven, that you may be a new lump. . . . Remove the wicked man from among yourselves" (1 Cor. 5:7,13). The purity of the church will be enhanced and preserved if those considering membership know they will be accountable to Christ's church and His under-shepherds for their actions. A person of shaky intentions is less likely to associate with a church if he knows his conduct may be subject to congregational discipline. Hopefully, this would not discourage committed Christians from church membership. It would, however, highlight the high standards of those who are members.

4. Growth encouraged

A fourth result of church discipline illustrated by the account of Ananias and Sapphira is church growth: "And all the more believers in the Lord, multitudes of men and women, were constantly added to their number" (Acts 5:14). Adherence to the principles of church discipline reflects a congregation's desire for personal godliness and strong commitment to the Lord's work. These are the seeds for church growth. As in Christ's analogy in John 15, the branches are pruned that they "may bear more fruit" (John 15:2). So in the work of the church, corrective discipline—"pruning"—enhances the atmosphere and attitudes necessary for aggressive church growth.

Restoring the backslider—James 5:19–20

At the conclusion of his epistle, James, the half brother of Jesus, encourages the brethren concerning the blessing of effective church discipline. James begins by acknowledging the possibility of a brother straying from the truth: "My brethren, if any among you strays from the truth . . ." (5:19). The words "among you" suggest that James is referring to a member of the believing community. James is saying it is possible for a brother or sister to fall into error—turning from the great doctrines of the Christian faith and the ethical conduct in keeping with one's position in Christ. Robertson points out that the third-class condition ("if") sets forth a supposed case, not assumed as true but yet probable.[3]

It is important for all Christians to realize it is *not* impossible for a brother or sister in Christ to wander from the truth. The Christian who thinks himself immune to temptation is a likely candidate for going astray. A lack of personal vigilance is often the first step to moral or doctrinal defection.

How should Christians respond to a believer who has gone astray? We can malign him. We can gossip about him. We can punish him and make him an example to others. We can kick him out of our church. Or we can exert ourselves and *restore* him. This last alternative is the one James suggests—". . . and one turns him back" (5:19). The priority of restoration is highlighted by Robertson:

> We are our brothers' keepers in spite of all they say and all that we may feel. You that are spiritual have a call to mind the broken lives all about you. There is no nobler work than this rescue work, to turn a sinner "from the error of his way."[4]

Tasker links this ministry with the mind of Christ and Christian love. He writes, "No duty laid upon Christians is more in keeping with the mind of their Lord, or more expressive of Christian love, than the duty of reclaiming the backslider."[5]

James does not outline for us how the restoration is to be brought about. But the focus on works and prayer in his epistle suggests that such restoration cannot be accomplished apart from faithful intercession and diligent effort.

How would a shepherd restore a wandering sheep to the sheepfold? He would seek out the lost sheep and find it. Then he would check the animal for injuries and anoint any wounds with oil. Then he would gently pick up the sheep and return it to the fold.

Paul would undoubtedly suggest an erring saint be reproved, corrected, and trained in righteousness through the ministry of the Word (2 Tim. 3:16, 17). Gentleness, compassion, mercy and healing are essential ingredients to any plan for church discipline where *restoration* is seen as the objective.

James 5:20 tells of the blessings achieved when a sinner re-

---

[3]A.T. Robertson, *Studies in the Epistle to James* (Nashville: Broadman Press, n.d.), p. 196.
[4]Ibid., p. 197.
[5]R.V.G. Tasker, *The General Epistle of James* (Grand Rapids: Wm. B. Eerdmans Publishing Co., 1956), p. 142.

sponds positively to the disciplinary process: "Let him know that he who turns a sinner from the error of his way will save his soul from death, and will cover a multitude of sins." It would be contrary to New Testament theology to regard the "soul" saved as that of the restorer rather than that of the reclaimed sinner. James commends works, but not as meritorious deeds obligating God's grace. The "soul" (v. 20) is that of the sinner who wandered from the truth.

There is considerable debate about the meaning of the expression "save his soul from death." Hiebert comments, "That he was saved *from death* stresses the seriousness of the condition from which he was rescued."[6] Some would understand "death" here to refer to physical death as divine discipline on sin (1 Cor. 11:30). Those who regard the backslider as unsaved suggest that he is saved from spiritual death—eternal separation from God. But since the backslider under consideration is seen to be a member of the Christian community ("any among you"), he is probably saved. The "death" from which he is delivered would best be regarded as *temporal* rather than *eternal* separation from God, for in this context "soul" refers to the inner life of the man, particularly in his relationship with God (cf. Mark 8:35 where *psyche* is translated "life"). In other words, James is addressing the very serious matter of broken fellowship with God. As in James 1:15, he appears to be using the imagery of "death" to emphasize the destruction that lies at the end of the path for those who pursue a course of sin (cf. Rom. 6:16, 23; 8:6, 13; Prov. 7:21–23).

The other tremendous result of restoring an erring sinner is that a "multitude of sins" will be covered. The sins covered are those committed by the one who has wandered from the truth, not the sins of the one who reclaims him. The covering of sins does not suggest any supplementary atonement, for the issue in this text is restoration, not salvation. And nowhere in Scripture is there evidence that one's good deeds atone for one's sins. No meritorious works are here implied.

The key to understanding this "covering of sins" is found in Prov. 10:12: "Hatred stirs up strife, but love covers all transgressions." Love enables us to put sins out of sight, to overlook wrongs and insults. The Apostle Peter makes this same point in 1 Pet.

---

[6]D. Edmond Hiebert, *The Epistle of James: Tests of a Living Faith* (Chicago: Moody Press, 1979), p. 335.

4:8: "Above all, keep fervent in your love for one another, because love covers a multitude of sins." Paul says in 1 Cor. 13:5: "[love] does not take into account a wrong suffered."

James presents here the joy and blessing of the one who, according to Robertson, "throws the mantle of love over the sins of the repentant sinner."[7] The one who participates in such restoration also shares in the exultation of the angels who rejoice when the sinner repents and turns back to God (Luke 15:8). God can and does "cover" our confessed sins by treating them as though they had never been. A Christian who turns a backsliding believer back to God is used to further the divine purpose of His love.[8]

When Discipline Fails

Most people think "successful" church discipline means that through confrontation and correction, the sinner has repented and returned to fellowship with Christ and His church. Certainly no one would deny that genuine repentance and restoration to fellowship bear the mark of "success." Unfortunately, restoration does not always occur. Of the twenty-one pastors who presented case studies in church discipline, only eight reported cases which resulted in repentance and restoration. In the other thirteen, those under discipline refused to repent and either left the church or were excommunicated. The following five examples provided by pastors will illustrate that church discipline does not always result in repentance.

1. "An ordained man was caught in homosexual activities by the police. He would not repent so I took another elder with me, and there was only hostility. I brought it before the elders and then to the church. The church voted to revoke his ordination. The man has still not repented and is still very bitter."

2. "A believer of ten years left his wife and two children to move to his own apartment. Later it became common knowledge around town that he was seeing another woman. He was confronted by the pastor and then by several elders separately. He was asked to meet with the elder board. He did meet with the board, but quoted John 10:10b ('I have come that they might have life, and might have it abundantly') as his reason for leaving

---

[7]Robertson, *Studies in the Epistle to James,* p. 199.
[8]Tasker, *The General Epistle of James,* p. 144.

his wife. There has been no repentance."

3. "An older gentleman was divorcing his wife of two years because of incompatibility. I shared that the only reason there was incompatibility was because of sin on both partners' parts. There were some counseling sessions, and then all of a sudden, he refused any more counsel and divorced his wife. He was approached by several church leaders, but there was no repentance. The matter was finally brought before the church. The man has never returned."

4. "A missionary of notable accomplishment became sexually involved with a woman other than his wife. When this was discovered, he was confronted by church leaders. He first denied any wrongdoing, but when his sin became widely known, he excused his wrongdoing and refused to repent. He was eventually dismissed from his church. He divorced his wife and married his girlfriend. He is trying to work out numerous problems in his second marriage, but has yet to acknowledge his wrong."

5. "An elder's wife was involved in an affair with another married Christian man. We spent the better part of a year trying to call her to repentance—first as a pastoral staff, then a small group from the elders and deacons, then the entire church board. After no indication of repentance, we publicly read a short statement to the membership of the church indicating her removal from the life and ministry of the church until there was a desire for repentance and restoration."

Could these cases of church discipline be considered successful? That depends on how one defines success.

Success must be defined from God's perspective, not man's. A preacher ministers successfully when he faithfully delivers a Christ-exalting message from God's Word. The failure of some to respond to his message does not mean the preacher was unsuccessful in his ministry (Ezek. 3:19). In the same way, *successful church discipline occurs when biblical guidelines are followed,* whether or not the offender repents and is restored. (This does not imply that God no longer sorrows for the saint who has strayed. It simply means God fully approves of the discipline which was carried out by the church.) Church discipline may be considered successful when the following questions can be answered positively:

1. *Have the biblical procedures for church discipline (Matt. 18:15–20) been observed?* Even discipline that includes the final step (excommunication) must be considered "successful" if the teachings

of Scripture have been carefully followed.

2. *Have those in sin or error been warned of the consequences of their behavior?* The writer of Hebrews warns his recalcitrant readers, "It is a terrifying thing to fall into the hands of the living God" (Heb. 10:31). Ezekiel was commissioned as a watchman to warn both the wicked and the righteous (Ezek. 3:16–21). God held Ezekiel accountable for the faithful deliverance of His message, but not for the success or failure of the response. So also, Christians have a responsibility to confront sinners and warn them of the dangers of their actions. If we have done our job well, then our mission has been successful, even if repentance is refused.

3. *Have the Christian leaders (those in authority, such as pastors or elders) acted responsibly?* Peter encourages the elders to "shepherd the flock of God among you" (1 Pet. 5:2). Shepherding involves feeding, guiding and protecting the sheep. It involves searching for the lost sheep and attending to their injuries. Have genuine attempts been made to turn the straying sinners back to God? The writer of Hebrews exhorts Christians to "obey your leaders, and submit to them; for they keep watch over your souls, as those who will give an account" (Heb. 13:17). If the church leaders can give a good account of their disciplinary procedures before the Lord, then the discipline has been successful.

4. *Have the church leaders and those involved made the disciplinary process a matter of prayer?* In Matt. 18:19, 20 Jesus links prayer to the exercise of church discipline. Prayer for the offender is appropriate throughout all disciplinary procedures (1 John 5:16). Church leaders often begin the process of discipline before they have interceded in behalf of the errant saint. They jump into discipline before they are assured of having the mind of Christ. Those who prayerfully seek God's wisdom in exercising discipline may be confident that the decisions they make will reflect the will of God in heaven.

The success or failure of church discipline must ultimately be evaluated from God's perspective, not man's. If biblical procedures have been followed and sincere efforts have been made to confront and correct the sinning saint, such discipline meets with God's approval and has His blessing—even when repentance and restoration does not occur.

10

THE DISCIPLINE OF CHRISTIAN LEADERS

Noah got drunk. Abraham lied. David committed adultery and murder. Peter cut off a man's ear. Euodia and Syntyche couldn't get along. Diotrephes usurped authority. The record of Scripture is quite clear. Spiritual leaders are not perfect. They sometimes sin.

This truth was driven home to me during my first year at seminary when I learned that the pastor of a prominent Baptist church in our area had been carrying on an immoral relationship. One morning in chapel an announcement was made that this well-known pastor had "fallen and injured his head" and that he was resting in the hospital. The students were asked to pray for his recovery. Several weeks later we learned the truth: The "fall" had been a moral one, and the "injury" was to the man's reputation. The pastor had been caught in the act of adultery. When his sin was discovered, he left town and never returned.

That a respected preacher and "man of God" could fall into such sin shocked me, a young, naive seminarian. Now, to my regret, I realize how common such sin is among Christian leaders. Sexual misconduct is one of Satan's favorite traps for Christian leaders. It destroys the preacher's confidence in addressing the issue of sin and smooths the way for a host of other compromises. But sexual immorality is not the only trap Satan uses. His arsenal includes alcohol abuse, financial impropriety, marital failure, pride, and uncontrolled anger.

One of the more unusual accounts of leadership failure took place in the New Testament Baptist Church of Stockton, California, where a minister allegedly shot and critically wounded a deacon who had disliked his sermon! According to the police,

Oscar MacAlister interrupted the Sunday morning sermon to tell Pastor Murphy Lee Paskell he was "getting out of hand." After the service, Paskell reportedly pulled a revolver and shot MacAlister four times. The pastor was booked by police on charges of attempted murder.

That Christian leaders are capable of sinning comes as no surprise to God. Anticipating this problem, He has provided clear instruction in His Word for the discipline of fallen Christian leaders.

The High Standards for Leaders

Theodore Roosevelt once said, "No man can lead a public career really worth leading, no man can act with rugged independence in serious crises, nor strike at great abuses, nor afford to make powerful and unscrupulous foes, if he is himself vulnerable in his private character."[1] If this is true of those who serve in public office, how much more applicable are these words with respect to those who serve in religious office. Both the Old and New Testaments set forth high standards for people in positions of spiritual leadership.

Treating God as holy—Lev. 10:1–11

The central theme of Leviticus is the holiness of God and the consequent holiness of His people. The theme of holiness is clearly seen in Leviticus 8–10, which records the consecration of the levitical priests. The priests represented the people before the Lord and had the closest contact with the holy things of Yahweh. Before beginning their duties, the priests were set apart in a special ceremony of consecration. They were first cleansed with water and then adorned in their priestly attire. Afterward they were anointed with oil and four sacrifices were offered in their behalf. For seven days after their consecration the priests remained in the tabernacle. This isolation intensified their consecration and emphasized their separation from the world.

Shortly after the inauguration of the levitical sacrifices, the priestly sons of Aaron learned an important lesson on God's demand for holiness. A violation of priestly ritual resulted in the fiery deaths of Aaron's two oldest sons: "Now Nadab and Abihu,

---

[1]C.T. Harnsberger, ed. *Treasury of Presidential Quotations* (Chicago: Follett Publishing Co., 1964).

the sons of Aaron . . . offered strange fire before the LORD, which He had not commanded them. And fire came out from the presence of the LORD and consumed them, and they died before the LORD" (Lev. 10:1–2).

Several explanations have been offered for the "strange" or "unauthorized" fire presented by Nadab and Abihu. Many suppose that the sin must have consisted in the fact that the fire for the incense was not taken from the incense altar (Lev. 16:12). Hence, it was "strange fire," not prepared in the proper way from the coals of the altar fire. Others suggest that they offered the incense at an improper time in response to the excited shouts of the people (Lev. 9:24; Ex. 30:9). The command in verse 9, taken in context, suggests that drunkenness may have caused the carelessness in presenting the sacrifice.

The lesson to be learned from this divine judgment upon the newly consecrated priests is found in verse 3. Moses quotes the Lord himself, saying, "By those who come near Me I will be treated as holy, and before all the people I will be honored." The words may literally be translated, "I must be sanctified among those who are near me, and I must be honored in the presence of the whole people."[2] The improper offering of Nadab and Abihu tainted God's reputation and thus required Him to vindicate His holiness before the people.

Wenham observes, "The whole nation was called to be holy, but how much more responsibility rested on the priests whose duty was to perform the sanctifying rituals and to teach the people the way of holiness."[3] The closer a person is to God, the more attention he must give to personal holiness to avoid injury to the glorious reputation of our Lord. Numerous Old Testament texts illustrate that spiritual leaders are judged by a higher, more exacting standard than those they lead (Num. 20:12; 1 Sam. 6:19; 1 Kings 13; 2 Kings 5:20–27; 2 Chron. 26:16–23).

Living above reproach—1 Tim. 3:1–7

The Old Testament is not unique in setting forth a high standard for those who occupy positions of spiritual leadership. According to Paul, the level of ethical purity demanded by the presence of God among believers is no lower for the church than it

[2]Gordon J. Wenham, *The Book of Leviticus* NICOT (Grand Rapids: Wm. B. Eerdmans Publishing Co., 1979), p. 155.
[3]Ibid., pp. 155–56.

was for ancient Israel (cf. 2 Cor. 6:14–7:1). He is agreeing with Jesus, who says, "And from everyone who has been given much shall much be required; and to whom they entrusted much, of him they will ask all the more" (Luke 12:48). James writes, "Let not many of you become teachers, my brethren, knowing that as such we shall incur a stricter judgment" (James 3:1).

In 1 Tim. 3, Paul instructs his young assistant, Timothy, regarding the appointment of church leaders at Ephesus. The discussion in verses 1–7 concerns the requirements for the office of "overseer" (*episkopes*). This term is used in Acts 20:17–28 and Titus 1:5–7 in synonymous relationship with the term "elder" (*presbuteros*). The term "overseer" emphasizes the function of the office—spiritual oversight. The term "elder" emphasizes the dignity of the office and the spiritual maturity required to occupy such a position. The more familiar term, "pastor" (Eph. 4:11), emphasizes the ministry of shepherding God's flock (Acts 20:28; 1 Pet. 5:2).

Paul says, "The overseer, then *must* be. . . ." (3:2). In other words, these standards are a basic minimum which must be met by any person holding a church office. Paul stresses the moral and spiritual qualities required of one in Christian leadership. The standards are admittedly high. But not every Levite could serve as a priest. And not every Christian meets the standards for church office. Certainly all believers should pursue the development of such qualities as Paul lists in 1 Timothy 3, but those who are church elders must meet the basic requirements.

Similar high standards are set forth for those holding the office of deacon (3:8–13). There is no suggestion in this passage that while the elders must be "spiritual men," the deacons can be less. Although not identical, the standards are parallel. Requirements for church office are as spiritually demanding for deacons as for elders.

The term "above reproach" (3:2) serves as the foundation for all the other qualifications. A similar term, "beyond reproach," is used of deacons in 1 Tim. 3:10 and of elders in Titus 1:6, 7. These terms imply character which is not open to criticism or accusation. The Christian leader must possess a "good reputation," and deservedly so. The terms do not mean that the elder must be perfect or sinless. If they did, no one could be totally above reproach this side of heaven. "Above reproach" means that the elder is consistently living in accordance with God's standards for Christian ethics and attitudes.

If a Christian leader is not "above reproach," he must be removed from office. Such removal may be temporary or permanent, depending on the nature of the failure and the attitude of the leader.

Many would like to compromise the high standards set forth for Christian leaders in 1 Timothy 3. We all have heard their arguments: "He is just a man of flesh, as are all of us." "Who of us is without sin?" "What would we be without him?" "We ought not to be so judgmental." "If the standards are *that* absolute, no one will qualify for church office."

These arguments imply that God cannot get along without us. That He has to get along with any available material. That He uses unqualified leadership because he can't get His purposes accomplished otherwise. What an inadequate view of God! Have we forgotten He is the Creator and Sustainer of the universe? While God allows us the honor of sharing in a little of what He is doing, He can get along quite well without us.

These statements also suggest that God is a pragmatist: That if it works, He will do it. That He is more interested in our activities than the quality of our lives. That He is more concerned about outward appearances than spiritual realities. This is not the God of the Bible. The true God is more concerned about the development of our spiritual beings—conformity to the image of Christ—than with anything we might do or accomplish for Him. He has His priorities straight. Do we?

The Discipline of a Leader

A pastor is arrested for soliciting a prostitute. An elder is found guilty of income tax evasion. An ordained seminary student leaves his wife to live with another student's wife. What instructions does God's Word provide for disciplining fallen Christian leaders?

Although Paul set forth high standards for church leaders (1 Tim. 3:1–7, 8–13), he knew those leaders would not be immune to sin. In 1 Tim. 5:19–22 Paul provides guidelines for situations in which the discipline of a Christian leader appears necessary. Paul's instruction builds upon Jesus' general instruction in Matt. 18:15–20, but here he addresses the more specific situation of a sinning leader.

The need for caution—5:19

While the elders who rule well are to be considered worthy of double honor (5:17), sometimes they receive just the opposite. People will often malign one with whom they disagree. Facts are distorted. Statements are exaggerated. Several years ago I received a call from a former student asking if it was true that I had divorced my wife. He had been informed by a bookstore manager that the author of *The Divorce Myth* had recently been divorced! I assured him that I was still very happily married and asked him to help me put an end to this false rumor. Fortunately, the false statement was corrected and there was no damage to my reputation. But the incident illustrates how easy it is for a Christian leader to be maligned by false accusations.

The pastors surveyed for this book expressed concern that precautions be taken against charging a pastor falsely. "You must have reliable witnesses." "Act on facts, not hearsay or rumor." "Make certain of the accuracy of the charge." "Get the facts straight before initiating action."

Charles Reagan, pastor of the First Baptist Church in Chippewa Falls, Wisconsin, observes, "The discipline of a church leader is the most serious kind of discipline." In light of the seriousness of this issue, it is crucial that we follow the scriptural guidelines, proceed slowly, and pray persistently when disciplining a Christian leader. Veteran pastor Dr. Jack MacArthur adds, "And be certain your attitude is Christlike."

Paul cautions Timothy and the church at Ephesus, "Do not receive an accusation against an elder except on the basis of two or three witnesses" (5:19). The requirement of two or three witnesses is founded on the Mosaic command (Deut. 17:6) which Christ reiterates in Matt. 18:16. The purpose of the witnesses is to present sufficient evidence for proceeding with disciplinary action against the elder. If sufficient evidence is lacking, no such action should be pursued or contemplated. Kent comments that this safeguard is a wise one: "No person is more subject to Satan's attack in the form of gossip and slander than God's servant."[4] Lenski rightly observes: "The honor due to the office demands this protection, for even a charge of which an elder is acquitted nevertheless damages his office and his work to some degree."[5]

---

[4]Homer A. Kent, Jr. *The Pastoral Epistles* (Chicago: Moody Press, 1958), p. 185.
[5]R.C.H. Lenski, *St. Paul's Epistles to the Colossians, Thessalonians, Timothy, Titus and Philemon* (Minneapolis: Augsburg Publishing House, 1961), p. 684.

The necessity of rebuke—5:20

The precaution of verse 19 is not designed to protect elders who have failed to live up to the high standards of their office. If the evidence of the witnesses is clear and convincing, then disciplinary action must be pursued: "Those who continue in sin, rebuke in the presence of all, so the rest may be fearful of sinning" (5:19). Literally the verse reads, "Those who are sinning, rebuke before all, in order that the rest may have fear." There is some debate as to whether the public rebuke should be reserved for those who *persist* in sinning or be applied also to the elder who is guilty of only *one* sin.[6]

The translation of the NASB has been construed to suggest that a public rebuke is to be reserved for those who "steadily persist" in sin after being privately confronted on several occasions. Therefore, a genuinely repentant elder need not be publicly rebuked. Proponents argue that the present active tense participle, *hamartanontas*, should be translated, "continue sinning."

Others interpret the present participle as merely descriptive, suggesting that the occasion of any well-attested sin would call for public rebuke. No distinction would be made between those who have repented and those who continue sinning. Paul is therefore contrasting those found innocent with those found guilty. Those found innocent of sin must not be charged. Those found guilty are to be publicly rebuked.

There is some truth to both of these viewpoints. Can we find a balance between them? "Those who are sinning" are the elders whose sins, verified by reliable witnesses, have come to light. Those found innocent, of course, are not to be charged. Those found guilty are to be rebuked. The present participle, "those who are sinning," is set in contrast with "the elders who rule well" (5:17). Those who rule well are to be doubly honored. Those who default in their duties, bringing dishonor to the name of Christ by their sinful actions, are to be publicly rebuked.

The Jerusalem Bible gives a clear rendering of the original

---

[6]Lenski comments, "The present tenses of the participle and the imperative are iterative. They refer to cases that may occur. The participle does not mean "those who steadily keep on sinning" (p. 684). Robertson, on the other hand, calls attention to the present active participle (*tous hamartanontas*) and translates, "The [elders] who continue to sin" (*Word Pictures in the New Testament* vol. 4 [Nashville: Broadman Press, 1931], p. 589). Unfortunately, neither commentator offers supportive arguments for his grammatical decision.

text: "Never accept any accusation brought against an elder unless it is supported by two or three witnesses. If any of them are
at fault, reprimand them publicly, as a warning to the rest" (5:18–
19). The present tense of the participle suggests that one slip-up
or failure would not necessitate a public rebuke. But circumstances which reflect a regular failing or character deficiency
would demand that public discipline be administered.

Notice that Paul does not give a list of sins which require
discipline. He does not suggest that discipline of Christian leaders should be reserved for the gravest of offenses—adultery with
the church secretary, embezzlement of the missionary fund, or
getting drunk with the communion wine. He simply refers to the
"missing of the mark." Those who, as Christian leaders, fall short
of God's standard are liable for discipline.

A word of caution is appropriate here. Frequently church
members will want to get rid of their pastor and will accuse him
of preaching too long, neglecting visitation, or starting a new
program without church approval. While these issues must be
resolved, they are not biblical bases for church discipline. We
must make sure that the discipline is for a definite *sin*, not just a
difference of opinion, personal dislike or hurt feelings.

The word "rebuked" suggests a reproof which brings conviction. It is used in John 16:8 of the convicting work the Holy
Spirit performs toward the unbeliever. In legal contexts, the word
means "to cross-examine or question for the purposes of reproving, censuring or accusing." The emphasis in the original
text is on the *public* nature of the reproof ("in the presence of
all"). It may be that Paul is assuming the previous steps for discipline, as outlined by Jesus in Matthew 18, have been followed.
Or possibly he is setting aside the preliminary steps in view of
the office Peter held and the seriousness of the issue (cf. James
3:1; Luke 12:48). This latter view is probably more consistent
with Paul's public rebuke of Peter at Antioch (Gal. 2:14) and his
pointing out of the sin of Hymenaeus and Alexander (1 Tim.
1:20). Public discipline is appropriate, then, in cases where the
offense is of a public nature and the offender holds a church
office.

What would the public rebuke of a Christian leader involve?
It would depend, of course, on the spiritual state of the fallen
leader. If genuine repentance has taken place, the "public rebuke" would function more as a "public acknowledgment" of the
sin *and the repentance* that has taken place. This may involve a

special church meeting where the failure is confessed and the church unites itself in prayer for the restoration of the fallen soldier. It would be necessary to relieve the elder of his ministry responsibilities until he reestablishes the congregation's trust and his own credibility and reputation. If repentance has not taken place, the rebuke may involve the exposure of the sin, verbal reproof by witnesses, exhortation to repentance, and removal of ordination.

Much prayer and loving concern must go into this disciplinary process, for the process is not to be vindictive, but restorative. Paige Patterson, director of the Criswell Center in Dallas, Texas, says, ". . . the church must do this with brokenhearted, conscientious concern over those being disciplined with the full understanding that the entire process involved in church discipline is designed to bring about restoration." A rebuke is restorative when it has the offender's best interests at heart and is designed not to punish, but to bring healing. A rebuke is restorative when it moves "beyond forgiveness" and begins the process of rebuilding the fallen Christian leader.[7]

It is not necessary to provide a detailed account of the transgression when rebuking a Christian leader. Paul points out that "it is disgraceful even to speak of the things which are done by them in secret" (Eph. 5:12). The church should not cater to the morbid curiosity of people who want to know the intimate details of a pastor's moral failing—the number of affairs or names of the women involved. The public disclosure of the specific nature of a sin such as homosexuality or incest makes it more difficult for some to forgive. Knowing the details of a pastor's sin may be neither edifying nor helpful. Restraint and caution ought to be observed.

Public discipline is not designed to shame and humiliate the offender, though it might. Paul intends that it serve to heighten the ethics of other Christians ("in order that the rest may have fear"). It is debated whether the "rest" (also "all") refers to the other elders or to the whole congregation. The latter viewpoint, of course, would include the former. Those who witness discipline before the congregation are led to reflect on their own lives and how dangerously close they often come to falling headlong into sin. A good, healthy fear of sin and its consequences is re-

---

[7]For a fine illustration of a restorative rebuke, see Don Baker's *Beyond Forgiveness* (Portland, Oregon: Multnomah Press, 1984), pp. 51–60.

stored to a congregation and its leaders when they observe discipline.

Some time ago a Christian leader I know and respect fell into sin and was disciplined by his church. My close association with that situation stirred my heart as never before to pursue a closer relationship with the Lord. Acknowledging how close I had sometimes come to spiritual disaster, I committed myself to spending more time with the Lord and pursuing a more godly life. I have sought all the more to keep my mind and conscience clean and to avoid the entanglements of sin. Although motivated in part by my love for God, I was catapulted out of my spiritual lethargy by fear of the shameful exposure and public discipline.

The demand for impartiality—5:21

Paul points out in the next verse that discipline must be administered with complete fairness and justice—without prejudice or partiality. He demands serious consideration of these matters: "I solemnly charge you in the presence of God and of Christ Jesus and of His chosen angels, to maintain these principles without bias, doing nothing in a spirit of partiality" (5:21).

The word "bias" refers to prejudgment—arrival at a decision before all the facts are in. The term "partiality" refers to an inclination toward someone. The discipline of Christian leaders is to be judicious and impartial. A leader, because of sentiment, should not be subject to lighter discipline than another person. It is very easy to respond with our emotions and be more generous in dealing with a leader we love and admire than with others. Probably in no other situation do we see such an expression of our human weakness, either in being overly harsh or in being overly lenient. Those involved in administering church discipline must be neither.

The restoration to leadership—5:22

In verse 22 Paul warns Timothy to exercise caution in associating himself with the ministry of another: "Do not lay hands upon any one too hastily and thus share responsibility for the sins of others; keep yourself free from sin." The concept of "laying on hands" may be traced to the Old Testament sacrificial system. When an animal was presented for sacrifice, the Israelite worshiper would lay his hands on the head of the animal in symbolic identification with the sacrifice (Lev. 1:4; 3:2; 4:4). By so doing, the worshiper would be saying, "This animal represents me; this animal shall die in my place; this animal's blood shall be shed for *my* sins."

The "laying on of hands" was used in the early church to signify the ordaining of ministers who would represent the church in missionary outreach. When Paul and Barnabas set off from Antioch on their first missionary journey, the members of the church "laid their hands on them" (Acts 13:3, cf. 6:6). The congregation was saying in essence, "Paul and Barnabas represent the church at Antioch. They are our hands, feet, and mouths in the world outreach."

In 1 Tim. 5:22 Paul warns Timothy that to lay hands on someone hastily might result in "sharing fellowship with the sins of others." Those who ordain share responsibility for the activities and ministry of those they commend to church office. When spiritual or moral failure takes place, guilt—to some extent—must rest upon the ordainers.[8] Paul encourages similar caution in the appointment of deacons (3:10).

Many expositors, following the lead of Chrysostom, have taken the view that Paul is speaking (v. 22) of the initial appointment of an elder. In other words, Paul is warning against a hasty ordination: "Wait," says Paul, "until you are sure of this man's character and qualifications, so you can avoid associating yourself with the sin of an erring elder." Certainly one way to avoid the painful experiences of church discipline is to be careful about who is ordained in the first place.

While there is wisdom in such precautionary measures *before* an initial ordination, the context of discipline (5:19–21) suggests that Paul is referring to the hasty restoration of a penitent elder to his former position.[9] The qualifications and matters concerning the appointment of elders were discussed rather thoroughly in 1 Timothy 3. In 1 Tim. 5:22 Paul is assuming that restoration of a repentant elder to a position of ministry is *possible*. Nonetheless, due precaution is required. The genuineness of the man's repentance must be determined. His reputation, credibility and trust must be restored.

After a parenthetical remark regarding Timothy's health and

---

[8]Kent, *The Pastoral Epistles*, p. 187.
[9]Walter Locke, *A Critical and Exegetical Commentary on the Pastoral Epistles* ICC (New York: Charles Scribner's Sons, 1924).

Paul's prescription, a reason is offered for caution in the matter of laying on hands (5:24–25). The sins of some men are clearly evident, disqualifying them immediately from office. With others, their disqualification by sin or misdeed is revealed only over time.

This brings us to an important principle in the matter of restoring Christian leaders. Restoration takes *time*. If the service station attendant gives me directions which result in my getting lost, it will be a long time before I trust his directions again. If a husband commits adultery, it will require a long period of faithfulness to restore his wife's trust. Similarly, sufficient time must pass for a disciplined Christian worker to be tried and proven. The leader who has fallen must once again earn the reputation of being "above reproach." It took years of faithful Christian living to qualify the first time. It may take that long to re-qualify for leadership after a fall.

There is another reason for allowing time to pass before restoration to leadership. (This may sound unspiritual, but the problem is real.) While a hyper-critical attitude or bitter spirit must not be tolerated, we must respect the strong feelings and emotions of those who believe they have been deceived by a sinning Christian leader. Realistically, it takes people some time to genuinely forgive and accept a brother who has been involved in gross sin. Healing takes time. We need to work toward restoration, but as Christian leaders, we need to move people gently. We must lead the sheep, not drive them by force, power, or authority to receive back a fallen shepherd before their hearts are ready (1 Pet. 5:2).

There is a sense in which the church must restore the leader. But there is also a sense in which the leader must restore himself. He must restore his reputation. He must restore his credibility. He must restore trust in the minds of those whom he has failed. This won't happen overnight. Opportunity must be provided for the brother to demonstrate his recommitment to the Lord by fulfilling tasks which do not involve leadership or public ministry. It took time to earn people's trust initially. It will take time to restore it after sin and deception.

The Restoration of a Leader

Madalyn Murray O'Hair, the famous crusader for atheism, made the cynical comment, "The church is the only army who shoots their own wounded." Although the statement is untrue, like many exaggerations it is based on a kernel of truth. The greatest failure in church discipline is the matter of restoration. The major goal of church discipline is to restore sinning saints. This is no less true when the saint who sins is in a position of leadership.[10] Christians who "shoot their wounded" are motivated by the flesh, not the Spirit. Those who neglect the healing process will never experience the blessedness of seeing a sinner restored to usefulness.

Upon learning of my interest in the subject of church discipline, a former seminary student wrote me about his own experience with church discipline. His letter, which follows, underscores the need to actively pursue the restoration of a fallen church leader.

> In June 1977, Helen and I returned home from two years of teaching in Ethiopia. Our home church had just called a new pastor, and he had begun his ministry just two weeks before we arrived home. When we got home, Helen and I hit it right off with the new pastor and his family. We became very close friends. Weekly, we did things together as families. I spent much time with him, and he was instrumental in directing me into the ministry. But within six months of his coming, he was gone.
>
> It was discovered that he was carrying on an affair with the secretary of his former church. He denied it against overwhelming evidence. He resigned, left the church, the state, and the ministry.
>
> I have never seen him since the day he left, but my heart aches every time I think of him. I wish I could sit down with him today and tell him how much I love and care for him. I was immature in many ways back then. Essentially, I turned my back on him during his greatest need.
>
> If I could do it over today, I would hold onto him and not let him self-destruct. I would love him even when he didn't want it. I would spend as much time with him as I could to help him work it through. I hurt and ache today thinking of the kind of friend and brother (Prov. 17:17) I should have been to my pastor. I long for the day when we will see each other in glory and all things will be new.

These words have caused me to reflect on the church's responsibility to come to the aid of a leader who has fallen into sin.

---

[10]See Erwin W. Lutzer's challenging article, "Restoring the Fallen," *Moody Monthly* (June 1984), pp. 106–107.

True restoration doesn't mean we ignore the sin or pretend it is less serious than it is. It doesn't mean we bypass the disciplinary process or fail to rebuke the offender. It doesn't mean we exercise mercy and neglect genuine guilt and accountability. But true restoration *does* mean we deal with a fallen leader in a Christlike manner—with compassion, forgiveness and genuine desire to assist in the healing process. It means we as church members and leaders come alongside the fallen warrior. To listen to his story. To encourage repentance. To offer assurance of forgiveness. To instruct from the Word. To pray for the rekindling of spiritual vitality.

After observing the discipline of a Christian leader, someone commented, "It is almost like a death." There is sorrow, regret and tears. The special fellowship once shared is now past. The disciplined leader is absent from his office. How should Christians respond? As in the case of seeing someone who has recently been bereaved, we don't know what to say or how to act.

No matter what our feelings, we must respond with love and Christlike concern. We should make contact with the fallen warrior as soon as possible to urge repentance, or express forgiveness if he has already repented. Comments about the leader's failing should be made with caution if we know something about him that is of a private, personal nature. We must be sensitive. We must avoid being flippant or trite.

When a leader falls, rebuke him. When he repents, restore him. The restoring congregation may collectively comprise a single powerful word from God concerning His forgiving love. By sharing in the restoration process, believers may become the sutures for closing self-inflicted wounds and the medicine for the process of recuperation. Forgiving Christians may be the servants of God in ministering to a fallen brother and a display of the glory of God in His justice and compassion. Christians can share in this kind of healing process if they will make restoration an integral part of the process of discipline.

Isn't it time that we recognize restoration not only as a possibility, but also as a priority in the exercise of church discipline?

11
THE DANGERS OF CHURCH DISCIPLINE

"Church, not mother sinned," announced the *Oregonian* headline on Friday, March 16, 1984. That was the verdict of a Tulsa, Oklahoma jury which decided a lawsuit against the Collinsville Church of Christ and three of its elders for "inflicting emotional distress and invading the privacy" of a woman disfellowshiped from the congregation. The jury awarded Marian Guinn $205,000 in actual damages and $185,000 in punitive damages following the week-long trial. The decision will be appealed to the Oklahoma Supreme Court. In light of the crucial issue of "free exercise of religion" stated in the First Amendment, the proverbial separtion of church and state, the case will probably come before the U.S. Supreme Court.

The Story of Marian Guinn[1]

Marian Guinn, a divorced mother of four, came to Collinsville, Oklahoma, in 1974. She had no money, no job, no skills, and only a two-year high-school education. She moved in with her sister and brother-in-law and struggled to get on her feet. Her sister was a member of the Church of Christ. Marian soon joined the same church and began attending services regularly. She secured a job, found a home for herself and her children, and went to night classes to finish high school. She then went on to community college and nursing school.

During the years that Marian was working on her education, members of the Church of Christ helped her with babysitting,

---

[1]The details of the story are taken from CBS's *60 Minutes* and an interview with Ted Moody, an elder of the Collinsville Church of Christ, reported in *The Christian Chronicle* 41 (April 1984), p. 21.

provided food and clothing for her family, and helped her in the purchases of two different cars. Says Ted Moody, an elder of the Collinsville church, "We adopted her and helped her like one would care for a daughter in need of assistance."

Trouble began in the summer of 1980 when Marian began dating former Collinsville mayor, Pat Sharp. Collinsville is a small rural town, so word of this relationship soon reached the ears of the church elders. The elders then met with Marian and told her Pat Sharp was not a suitable man for her to be seeing. They cautioned Marian about her involvement with Pat and where that involvement was leading.

In September of 1981 an incident occurred which started the final chain of events. For reasons of his own, Pat Sharp called one of the elders. Before the conversation was over, he admitted that he and Marian were having an affair. The elders met again with Marian and asked her if what Pat Sharp had told them was true. She admitted that it was. In another meeting with the elders, Marian agreed not to see Pat Sharp again. But she saw him three times afterward, though she had no sexual relations with him on those occasions.

On the evening of September 16, 1981, the elders heard that Marian was out again with Pat. They went to her home and waited in her driveway until she returned. The elders told Marian that she would have to repent publicly or they would have to announce her sin to the congregation and withdraw fellowship from her. On September 21, 1981, the elders sent Marian a letter urging her to repent and begin attending church services again. Marian responded with a letter which she hand-delivered on Sunday, September 27. Here is part of that letter:

> I do not want my name mentioned before the church except to tell them that I withdraw my membership immediately. I have never fully accepted your doctrine and never will. Anything I told you was in confidence and not meant for anyone else to hear. In view of your lack of concern regarding my children, I have no choice but for all of us to attend another church, another denomination, where men do not set themselves up as judges for God. He does His own judging.

Marian gave the letter to Ron Witten, a church elder, who read the letter in her presence.

He responded, "Marian, you can't withdraw from us. We have to withdraw from you."

Marian quoted Matt. 7:1, "Judge not lest you be judged" and

John 8:7, "Let he who is without sin cast the first stone." She was assured by Ron Witten that the verses did not apply in her situation.

The elders did not accept her resignation. Marian would remain a member until disfellowshipped by the church. That action was taken on the following Sunday, October 4, 1981. A letter was read to the congregation informing the members of the disciplinary action. Three reasons were given for this discipline: lack of attendance at services, fornication, and disobedience to the elders.

The disciplinary action taken by the Collinsville Church of Christ was reported to four neighboring churches. Two of those sister churches had been started by members of the Collinsville Church of Christ. The other two had numerous former members of the Church of Christ who had some association with Marian Guinn.

When Marian learned that the church had taken public action against her, she decided to take her stand. "What I do or do not do is between God and myself," she said. "I'm really upset that these men think they have the authority to mess with someone's life like that." Marian secured the services of attorney Thomas Frasier and filed a lawsuit against the church and three elders for 1.35 million dollars. The charges were "invasion of privacy and willful intention to inflict emotional distress." Prior to going to trial, the Collinsville elders appealed to the Supreme Court to throw the case out since the courts have no jurisdiction over church affairs. The Court refused to hear the case and it went to the district court in Tulsa in mid-March, 1984.

The View of Marian Guinn's Attorney

To Thomas Frasier, Marian's attorney, the acknowledged affair between his client and Pat Sharp is irrelevant to the case. "It doesn't matter if she was fornicating up and down the street," he insisted. "It doesn't give [the church] the right to stick their noses in" her private business.[2] In an interview on *60 Minutes*, Marian said she was told by the elders that her conversations with them "would be held in the strictest of confidence." She admitted under testimony during the trial, however, that she was sexually involved with Pat Sharp.

---

[2]*Newsweek* (February 27, 1984), p. 46.

According to Marian, she "did everything but get down on my knees" to avoid having her name brought before the congregation for public discipline. Guinn told the court, "I'm not saying I wasn't guilty. I was. But it was none of their business."[3] By resigning from membership, she had hoped to avoid the public humiliation that disclosure of her sin would involve.

According to her attorney, this is where the church erred. "If they had heeded her letter that they received on the 25th of September and allowed her to withdraw from fellowship of their 120-member church, we would not have initiated this action at all," said Frasier.

"I demand the right, on behalf of Marian Guinn, to lead her life the way she chooses to lead her life," Guinn's attorney said in his closing arguments. Frasier likened the church's action to that detailed in Nathaniel Hawthorne's *The Scarlet Letter*, in which the adulteress, Hester Prynne, is made to wear the letter *A* as punishment for her sin. In regard to her sexual relationship with Pat, attorney Frasier said, "He was a single man. She was a single lady. And this is America."[4]

The View of the Collinsville Elders

The church elders, Ron Witten, Ted Moody and Allen Cash, testified that they acted out of concern for Marian Guinn's spiritual life and her relationship with God. On *60 Minutes* one of the elders said, "We elders feel a grave responsibility to our sister Marian. We shepherd over her and we are concerned very much about her soul and her relationship with God. And it is through the love that we have had for Marian that through the years we were concerned about her soul's condition."

"She was guilty of fornication," said Ron Witten. "She was guilty of unfaithfulness in her attendance [at church]. She was guilty of disobeying the elders." The elders had counseled Marian to repent or the church would withdraw from her. She refused.

Truman Rucker, deacon at the Collinsville Church of Christ and church attorney, argued as the case was going to trial that Marian Guinn's personal life ceased to be a private matter once her affair became public knowledge. The pair's involvement had

[3]*Time* (March 26, 1984), p. 70.
[4]*The Oregonian* (March 16, 1984).

become "town gossip" over a period of months and had become a matter of concern for the church. "People had seen his car over at her house at night," Rucker explained. The elders had a responsibility to protect the church's reputation.[5] Rucker also pointed out that the elders acted out of "their love for Marian Guinn" and "had a sacred duty . . . to make sure her soul is right with God."

The elders testified during the trial that their actions were guided by a literal interpretation of Matt. 18:15–17 where Jesus Christ lays out the procedure for dealing with a wrongdoer. Their actions reflected the final step in dealing with an unrepentant offender: "And if he refuses to listen to them, tell it to the church; and if he refuses to listen even to the church, let him be to you as a Gentile and tax gatherer."

Church attorney Rucker said, "The elders have a sacred duty to watch over the flock, to help them overcome these types of problems." In the interview on *60 Minutes*, elder Ron Witten acknowledged that the church leaders were responsible before God for their discipline of Marian Guinn and would be held accountable if they neglected this sacred duty.

It was apparent from the church records that the elders were not "picking on" Marian Guinn. The withdrawal of fellowship is a method of enforcing moral values used fairly frequently in the Collinsville church, perhaps once every two or three years, Rucker said. The elders contended that Guinn's defense could not rest on the fact that she was not a member, since there is no scriptural precedent for quitting the church.

The announcement of the disciplinary action to the church on October 4, 1981, was filled with "emotion, heartache and grief," said Rucker. The church elders banned fellowship with sister Marian. A tape recording of the announcement was played in court. The elders told members "to withdraw fellowship from our sister in Christ, Marian Guinn." Withdrawal of fellowship is the "last resort of discipline," elder Ted Moody testified.

But this discipline was designed to bring Marian to repentance. Elder Ron Witten said, "If Marian were to come back tomorrow, we would welcome her with open arms and the angels in heaven would join with us."[6]

---

[5]*Newsweek* (February 27, 1984), p. 46.
[6]*Time* (March 26, 1984), p. 70.

The View of the Jury

After hearing the various arguments during the four-day trial, the Tulsa jury sided with 36-year-old Marian Guinn, and the court awarded her $390,000 in actual and punitive damages. The amount is more than *six times* the Collinsville Church of Christ's annual budget.

"A wrong was made right," said a pleased Marian Guinn.

"Just because 12 people [the jury] don't understand the teachings of the church doesn't mean that we're guilty of harassment," said Ron Witten.[7] Truman Rucker, representing the elders, announced that the verdict would be appealed.

"Whether we pay or don't pay [the fine], we will be concerned about Marian until her life is made right with the Lord," said Allen Cash, one of the defendants. "It won't be a victory until Marian has returned to the Lord."[8]

Winnowing the Arguments

Winnowing is the procedure for separating the heads of grain from the bits of broken straw and foreign matter. As grain must be winnowed at harvest, so the arguments presented in the Guinn trial must be weighed and evaluated. The elders of the Collinsville Church of Christ were charged with "invading privacy" and "inflicting emotional distress" in connection with their discipline of Marian Guinn. How valid are these charges?

With regard to the "privacy" issue, it should be remembered that it was Marian herself, not the elders, who brought her conduct to the public's attention. According to biblical standards, she was involved in an immoral relationship. This fact was known by those in city hall and many other citizens of the Collinsville community. Also, the genuineness of Marian's concern over the issue of "privacy" seems doubtful in view of her willingness to be interviewed on *60 Minutes,* a very popular, nationwide television news program. Indeed, the public nature of her lawsuit against the church ultimately reflects the fact that "privacy" was not a preeminent issue with Marian Guinn.

With regard to the issue of "emotional distress," I do not doubt for a moment that Marian Guinn experienced plenty. No one with any kind of conscience could commit immorality, deny

---

[7] *The Christian Chronicle* 41 (April 1984), p. 1.
[8] Ibid.

the sinfulness of such actions, refuse to repent, be the subject of community scandal, be called to accountability by one's church and *not* experience some emotional distress. The key issue seems to be whether or not the emotional distress Marian Guinn experienced was brought upon her by the intentional actions of the elders.

From my reading on this case, I am fairly confident the elders were acting out of loving concern for Marian. They did not intend their actions to harass, bring personal harm or cause emotional distress. Marian's words on the witness stand reflected her own view that the elders did not act out of malice. She stated that she knew the elders had acted out of love for her.[9]

The elders of the Collinsville Church of Christ were doing nothing extraordinary in their dealings with Marian Guinn. There is solid scriptural basis and historical precedent for congregational discipline. The Constitution of the United States guarantees the free exercise of religion. In a Bible-believing church, part of that exercise includes the discipline of its members.

But someone asks, "What about Marian Guinn's rights?" Some would say that she was deprived of her rights. Responding to Mike Royko's scathing denunciation of the elders[10], Charles H. Totom (The Dalles, Oregon) addressed the issue of Guinn's rights. In a letter to the editor of the *Oregonian*, he said, "Guinn was not deprived of her right to religious freedom, nor was she deprived of her loose lifestyle. What she was forbidden was an immoral life style in the church."[11]

The action of the elders was necessary for Guinn's sake, that she would see the error of her way; for the church's sake, that the members would fear the consequences of sin and walk in holiness; and for the community's sake, that the people might know that God's church takes a stand against immorality in the lives of its members.

But are the elders of the Collinsville Church of Christ without fault? These men sincerely sought to exercise scriptural discipline, but it appears they overextended the bounds of their responsibility when they reported their actions to four neighboring congregations. Although it was argued that this was necessary because of the close association of these churches with the Col-

[9]*Christian Chronicle* 41 (April 1984), p. 21.
[10]"Jurors' verdicts decide disparate questions of sexual conduct," *Oregonian* (March 27, 1984).
[11]"Bible gives rights," *Oregonian* (April 7, 1984).

linsville Church of Christ, this could be interpreted as "harass-ment." It seems to have been an unwise decision.

Churches must at times cooperate when a member under discipline leaves a congregation to join another assembly. But in cases of that nature, the information given to another pastor must be private and at the request of the receiving congregation. Marian Guinn expressed no interest in joining another church in Collinsville, so cooperative discipline does not seem to have been necessary in her case.

It appears that the elders of the Collinsville Church of Christ may have lost track of the ultimate goal of church discipline—the restoration of the sinning saint. The purpose of the public announcement of the sin in the third step of discipline is to en-courage repentance and restoration (Matt. 18:17). By taking the church matter to other churches, a wedge was driven between the church and Marian Guinn, making it an unlikely chance she will ever return to the Collinsville Church of Christ, even if she repents. When questioned whether she thought the church would really "welcome her with open arms" if she repented, Marian replied, "I don't know if they would throw their arms around me or not. I don't intend to find out."

It is extremely unfortunate that this unpleasant matter could not have been dealt with in the local church rather than before the civil authorities. In 1 Cor. 6:5–6, Paul addresses the issue of lawsuits between Christians: "I say this to your shame. Is it so, that there is not among you one wise man who will be able to decide between his brethren, but brother goes to law with brother, and that before unbelievers?" Paul goes on to note, "Actually, then, it is already a defeat for you, that you have lawsuits with one another. Why not rather be wronged? Why not rather be defrauded?" (6:7). Even if the decision of the lower court is re-versed, there will be no "winner" in the Marian Guinn lawsuit. Both the accuser and the accused have been defeated by a dis-pute that has caused unbelievers such as Mike Royko to ridicule Christ's church.

The Issues at Stake

The court's decision in favor of Marian Guinn raises several significant questions: Does the civil government have the right to infringe on church procedures for disciplining its members? What does the future hold for churches which are seeking to exercise biblical discipline? What kind of societal morality does the outcome of the trial represent and reflect?

An editorial in the *Christian Chronicle* provides a significant observation about the trial: ". . . the trial pitted two lifestyles against each other and then said immorality was more acceptable in our society than a church pleading with an immoral, but beloved member to repent."[12]

Chuck Colson, president of Prison Fellowship, pointed out in *Jubilee*, the monthly newsletter of Prison Fellowship, that the Marian Guinn case presents two issues of enormous significance: The *first* is whether the state can hold the church liable for enforcing biblical standards on its members. The *second* is less obvious, but even more disturbing: The Guinn case tells us how the church is perceived by the culture.[13]

With regard to the first issue, if the decision of the Tulsa court stands, any Bible-believing church which exercises discipline may face a lawsuit. Colson remarks that this would be "an outrageous invasion by the state in the affairs of the church, and would reduce the church to nothing more than a Sunday morning Rotary Club."[14] The decision of the court appears to be a classic violation of the principle of "free exercise" of religion, the separation of church and state.

Addressing the second, more serious issue, Colson jolts us with a sobering thought: "As the world sees us, the church has no business being concerned with the moral standards of its members. Unfair? Or is the world's perception justified by the way we've acted?" Christian leaders must ask themselves some tough questions:

1. Have we become more concerned with enlistment and church membership than demanding righteousness and spiritual discipline?

2. Do we preach a prosperity gospel, or do we call our comfortable congregations to repentance?

3. Do we really insist that our faith make a difference in how we live—including not just piety but our views on justice, caring for the disadvantaged, even our perceptions of art, literature, music?[15]

---

[12]Howard W. Norton, "Editorial: Do We Kill Our Wounded?" *Christian Chronicle* 41 (April 1984), p. 22.

[13]Chuck Colson, "The Church Should Mind Its Own Business," *Jubilee* (April 1984), p. 3.

[14]Ibid.

[15]Ibid.

Colson points out that the world's perception of the church, as reflected in the court's decision, may not be far from the mark. "Our culture doesn't think morality is any of our business because they haven't seen us *make* it our business," says Colson.

In his concluding words, Chuck Colson makes this probing remark: "It will be bad news if the court should emasculate the church by holding that it can't enforce biblical standards on its members; but it will be even worse news if it turns out that by ignoring our biblical responsibilities we have done it to ourselves."[16]

Avoiding a Lawsuit

America is a happy hunting ground for those with "get-rich-quick" schemes. One scheme gaining prominence these days is the lawsuit. Traffic accident victims are suing automobile manufacturers. Injured skiers are suing ski resorts. Inmates are suing prison officials. Students are suing their teachers for failing to give a proper education. In one recent case a drunken driver ran his car into a stone monument in a city park, then sued the city for the injuries sustained in the accident—and won the case!

The specter of litigation now looms over our churches and church leaders. It is significant that five years ago Church Mutual Insurance Company, which has been insuring church buildings since 1898, added coverage up to one million dollars for clergy desiring protection from malpractice actions relating to their counseling of parishioners.[17] While it is probably impossible to avoid a lawsuit if a malicious person insists on pursuing that course of action, the chances of being sued for the exercise of church discipline can be reduced. The following principles were prepared in consultation with Samuel E. Ericsson, director of the Center for Law and Religious Freedom in association with the Christian Legal Society.

First, include a complete statement in your church constitution detailing the congregation's beliefs regarding church discipline. Outline the steps for church discipline and provide the scriptural basis for disciplinary procedures. State clearly that the Bible, as interpreted by the church leaders, will serve as the ultimate guide for church discipline.

---

[16]Ibid.

[17]John W. Montgomery, "Could Your Pastor Be Sued?" *Christian Life* (May 1981), p. 24.

Second, acquaint those seeking membership in your church with the constitution, including the church's procedures for dealing with sinning saints. Inform them that as members of the church, they will be expected to abide by the church constitution and submit to its requirements. Make certain they sign an agreement to abide by the constitution.

Third, include in your church constitution or covenant a statement to the effect that "we the members of _____ Church will not pursue legal action or sue the pastors, elders, deacons or church staff in connection with the performance of their official duties." Over the past 15 years U.S. Courts have held rather consistently in a variety of situations that an individual cannot waive his or her right to sue. Nevertheless, such a statement would probably serve as a deterrent against lawsuits. Most Christians would seek to honor such a promise. It may be well to include a general statement about your church's view on lawsuits based on 1 Cor. 6:1–8.

Fourth, when church discipline is necessitated, make sure that it is carried out in accordance with the church constitution. Strict adherence to the biblical steps for church discipline will deter charges of partiality, prejudice and intentional infliction of emotional distress.

Fifth, point out in the constitution that the members of the church have entered into a covenant together to tend to each other's spiritual needs and that this covenant agreement is to end only by the consent of the church leaders. This statement will guard against someone suing the church for administering discipline after "resignation from church membership."

Sixth, if information is disclosed to the pastor, elders or church leaders in confidence, such privileged information must not be disclosed to others. Sam Ericsson strongly emphasized this point in conversation on this issue. It is here that the Collinsville Church of Christ elders may have erred. Marian Guinn insisted that what she had told the elders was in strict confidence. When the elders reported to their own church and to several other churches details of Marian's private conversation, they exposed privileged and private information and were legally accountable.

Seventh, respect the privacy of the one being disciplined. Avoid any appearance that the the discipline is designed to harass or cause emotional distress. If public disclosure is necessary, consider carefully the wording of the announcement. It is possible to exercise public discipline without public exposure of privileged information. It is not always necessary to name the specific sin committed. A general statement may be sufficient. Motivated by loving concern and a desire for restoration, careful wording can be used to "tell it to the church" without violating confidence.

Eighth, do not make the discipline known outside the church family. Although the elders of the Collinsville Church of Christ thought it necessary, they appear to have overextended the bounds of their responsibility when they reported their actions to four neighboring congregations. There may be two exceptions to this guideline: (1) when another church inquires concerning the fitness for church membership of a disfellowshipped person, and (2) when an ordained minister's ordination is revoked. In the former situation all that need be said is, "John Doe did not leave our church in good standing. In view of his unrepentant heart, we cannot recommend him for membership in your church." In the latter situation, it would be prudent for such discipline to be announced to other churches *within* the denomination.

Ninth, if a lawsuit is filed against the church or church leaders, pursue an out-of-court settlement or an alternative means of resolving the conflict. The goal in procedures of mediation should be reconciliation, not "winning." The Christian Legal Society of Oak Park, Illinois, recently established the Christian Conciliation Services to help Christians in resolving legal disputes.[18]

A church may choose to pursue discipline in spite of the threat of a lawsuit. A pastor in the East discovered that one of his church members was involved in an illicit relationship. He went to the brother and lovingly sought to correct him. There was no response. Next, he took two of the church elders with him to rebuke the sinning brother. Still no response. He warned the brother that the next step would be to take the matter to the church for public discipline. The offender was enraged! This was his business—no one elses! He threatened the pastor and the church with a lawsuit if this personal matter was made public.

After carefully weighing the possible consequences, the pastor told the offender, "I love you too much to let you continue

[18]Samuel E. Ericsson, "How to Avoid a Lawsuit," *Christian Life* (May 1981), p. 27. See also Lynn R. Buzzard and Laurence Eck's *Tell It To The Church* (Elgin, Illinois: David C. Cook Publishing Co., 1982).

to sin against God and ruin your life. Sue us if you must, but we will follow biblical principles and take this matter to the church if you don't break off this sinful relationship." It was a bold and self-sacrificing step. But it was effective in encouraging the offender to repent. And, thankfully, no lawsuit was filed.

Church discipline is dangerous. In spite of all our precautions, your church and its leaders may still be sued. But if you have followed biblical procedures and administered discipline out of love and with a view to restoration, you can have a clear conscience before God regardless of the outcome of the trial. Such an experience would give one a much greater appreciation of Paul's words in 2 Tim. 3:12: "And indeed, all who desire to live godly in Christ Jesus will be persecuted."

12
CHURCH DISCIPLINE IN AMERICA

The seventeenth-century English philosopher, John Locke, wrote, "If we rightly estimate what we call good and evil, we shall find it lies much in comparison." The deceptiveness of making comparisons can be illustrated by the story about the little boy who came running to his mother one day and said, "Mother, guess what! I'm eight feet four inches tall!" Upon investigating the matter, his mother discovered the boy was using a six-inch ruler. What a disappointment it was for him to learn he was only four feet two inches tall.

We often measure ourselves using each other as a standard, and conclude we are doing well—"At least I'm not like so-and-so!" Thus we reassure ourselves. But the problem is that we are using the wrong measuring stick. We must measure ourselves, not by the standard of human achievement, but by the standard of the Word of God.

It is therefore not my purpose in this chapter to present the norm as the standard. In response to my survey, one pastor wrote, ". . . it seems to me that a survey of what pastors and church leaders believe and do is of relevance only to those who are impressed with or (worse) governed by norms. This represents a terribly average sort of morality. . . ." This is quite true. But I do not intend here to set the standard, but to determine where we are with respect to *the* standard—God's Word.

Having carefully researched the teaching of Scripture on church discipline, it would be helpful to survey pastors from the major Protestant denominations to determine their thoughts and attitudes on this subject. We can also benefit greatly from their collective wisdom and experience in dealing with church discipline. My primary objective here is to give Christian leaders a sense of "the state of the church" in America with respect to church discipline. Most would agree that we are falling short of the biblical standard. But how short are we falling? What are the major difficulties in administering church discipline? I asked 1,300 pastors to tell me. This chapter analyzes their replies.

The Selective Survey

My research actually involved two surveys. The first was a trial run to test the survey instrument and begin gathering illustrative information. On January 30, 1984, I sent a survey to 48 pastors and Christian leaders whom I selected on the basis of personal acquaintance and prominence in leadership. I received 38 completed surveys, a return of 79 percent.

The primary benefit of this first survey was the helpful insights and suggestions of many seasoned pastors who have struggled for years with church discipline. Their combined experience, along with the personal illustrations they provided, have contributed greatly toward the research and writing of this book. Their insightful comments and stories are found throughout these chapters. The "trial run" survey also pointed out several questions that needed to be simplified and improved. And the fact that 5 of the 38 respondents did not write their names on the survey indicated that the random survey should be anonymous.

The Random Survey

To prepare the random sample, I contacted the main office or headquarters of the 112 Protestant denominations in North America having ten thousand or more members.[1] The *Yearbook of American and Canadian Churches 1983* served as the resource for membership statistics.[2] I explained my survey to the denominational representatives and requested denominational directories or lists of present pastors so that names could be selected on a random sample basis.

Fifty-five of the denominational headquarters responded by sending the lists I requested. From the directories and lists provided me, 1,250 names were selected. I determined the number

---

[1] There were some exceptions. I did not contact the headquarters of Protestant churches which clearly fall outside the ranks of Christian orthodoxy.

[2] Constant H. Jacquet, Jr., ed. (Nashville: Abingdon Press, 1983), pp. 224–31.

of names from each group in proportion to the size of the denomination. The larger denominations received more surveys; the smaller denominations received fewer. The surveys were mailed out May 14, 1984. A stamped, self-addressed envelope was provided to return the completed survey.

Of the 1,250 mailed out, 439, or 35 percent, of the surveys were returned as of July 31, 1984. Experts say this is a satisfactory response for a voluntary random sample survey.

In presenting the survey, I did not define "church discipline" for the respondents. In view of the differing backgrounds of those surveyed, I determined it would be better to leave room for a flexible interpretation of what church discipline includes. I introduced the survey with a letter asking for assistance in this research project. The following paragraph was placed at the beginning of the survey:

> This anonymous, random survey will provide data essential to discovering what pastors and Christian leaders in America are thinking regarding church discipline. Your participation is essential to making this research project a valuable study.

Responses to the survey varied. One apparently frustrated pastor remarked, "Dr. Laney, this is a dumb survey." Another commented, "Glad to help; this subject needs attention. Thanks."

The pastors sampled

The pastors sampled came from a broad spectrum of denominations and theological persuasions. The largest groups of respondents represented the following: United Methodist (70); Southern Baptist (61); those who simply labeled themselves "Baptist" (46); Missouri Synod Lutheran (20); the American Lutheran Church (19); the Lutheran Church in America (18); those who simply identified themselves as "Lutheran" (22); the Assemblies of God (21); no denomination indicated (61).

The remainder of the 439 surveys came from pastors of such denominations as the Wesleyan Church, Church of God, Free Methodist, Christian Church, Church of the Nazarene, Salvation Army, Moravian, Conservative Baptist, Seventh-Day Adventist, Christian and Missionary Alliance, Mennonite, Church of the Brethren, Foursquare, Presbyterian Church in America, Church of Christ, General Association of Regular Baptists and many more.

The respondents displayed impressive personal character and ministry experience. These pastors were mature Christian leaders with an average of 23.5 years in the ministry. Their responses and comments showed a sincere concern for people and their spiritual needs.

Results of the survey

The questions asked on the survey and the responses received are reported as follows. Each percentage represents the portion of the 439 pastors and Christian leaders who responded to the survey.

1. *Which of the following would serve to guide your congregation in administering church discipline?*

> Local church constitution 41.11%
> Denominational bylaws 31.48%
> Local church leaders 18.89%
> The Bible 6.11%
> No guidelines 2.40%

Comments: The Bible was a "write-in" since it was not provided as an option for the responders. Perhaps more would have mentioned it had it been listed among the options. The church constitution is looked to most frequently for guidance in the administration of church discipline. Hence, it is probably the best place to address the matter and outline disciplinary procedures.

2. *How would you evaluate your ability to deal with situations which require church discipline?*

> Poorly equipped 5.65%
> Not quite adequate 14.35%
> Adequate 37.41%
> Capable 31.06%
> Quite competent 11.53%

Comments: The respondents rated themselves just slightly above "adequate" in their ability to deal with situations which require church discipline. The Assemblies of God pastors gave themselves the highest rating ("capable"). Next came the United Methodists and the Lutherans. The Baptists trailed the others rating themselves "adequate."

The pastors and Christian leaders surveyed rated their ability to handle church discipline higher than I expected. In evaluating this data, I believe that if the question was placed at the end—rather than the beginning—of the survey, the evaluations would not be quite so high. Sometimes a respondent marked "quite competent" or "capable," but the next question revealed that the minister had very little if any experience in church discipline beyond that of private correction or reproof.

3. *How frequently have you had to initiate or be involved in the following kinds of church discipline? Please estimate: 1—never; 2—several times; 3—once a year; 4—once a month.* (The figures recorded below represent the average number of times a typical responder has participated in the various forms of church discipline based on the preceding scale.)

Private correction or reproof: Participated several times (2.27)
Reproof with witnesses: Participated several times (1.82)
Disclosure to the church leaders: Participated several times (1.84)
Disclosure to the church members: Participated never (1.30)
Withold participation in communion: Participated never (1.14)
Removal from office or position: Participated never—several times (1.61)
Excommunication from the church: Participated never (1.20)

Comments: The Assemblies of God respondents had the highest frequency of participation in church discipline, averaging "several" involvements (1.98) for the disciplinary measures listed. The Baptists came next with an average of "never to several" (1.63), followed by the Lutherans with 1.54 and the United Methodists with 1.38. One United Methodist pastor commented, "This kind of 'discipline' is not generally a part of U.M. practice."

4. *Of the cases of church discipline you have observed or been involved with, approximately what percent were successful in restoring the offender to fellowship with God and the congregation?*

The average success rate for restoration following discipline was 51.57 percent of the cases. I was surprised and encouraged that over half of the instances of church discipline resulted in restoration. Yet that means that in almost half the cases where church discipline was applied, it *failed* to bring about restoration. There remains much work to close this gap. Although the survey did not elicit such data, it would be interesting to know the *kinds* of discipline (see question 3) which were most effective. It is obvious that the 50 percent success rate is not a result of excommunication or forbidding participation in communion since these forms of discipline are rarely practiced.

5. *If a church leader (pastor, elder, deacon) is found to be engaging in*

immoral conduct, but confesses and repents, how do you view that person's future ministry? (The percentages represent the portion of the respondents checking each option.)

(1) Never again qualified for church leadership: 3.30%
(2) May be qualified again after a period of discipline: 19.63%
(3) May return to office upon restoration of credibility and trust: 67.36%
(4) May continue in church leadership without interruption: 9.71%

Comments: The average response fell between the second and third option (2.84) indicating that most responders viewed restoration to ministry as a possibility after a period of discipline or upon restoration of credibility and trust. In the light of Gal. 6:1, it is encouraging to see such a positive view on the possibility of restoration to ministry. Yet, those surveyed recognized that due caution must be observed.

There was only a very slight difference of opinion among the Methodists (3.01), Lutherans (2.96) and Baptists (2.94) on the matter of restoration. The Assemblies of God pastors appear to be somewhat more strict (2.3) in their procedures for restoration to ministry.

Questions 6–10 are rated on a scale of 1–4 with values as follows: 1—Never; 2—Seldom; 3—Sometimes; 4—Always. In attempting to simplify the results for the reader, I have adopted the following categories:

Never = 1.00–1.24
Almost never = 1.25–1.49
Rarely = 1.50–1.74
Seldom = 1.75–2.24
Occasionally = 2.25–2.49
Sometimes = 2.50–2.79
Often = 2.80–3.24
Frequently = 3.25–3.49
Almost always = 3.50–3.74
Always = 3.75–4.00

6. *How often do the following thoughts and feelings enter your mind when you are called upon to administer church discipline?*

Pain: Almost always (3.58)
Dread: Often (3.21)
Anxiety: Frequently (3.33)
Restoration: Almost always (3.70)

Healing: Almost always (3.68)
Sorrow: Almost always (3.61)
Opportunity: Often (3.10)
Anger: Occasionally (2.43)
Compassion: Almost always (3.65)

Comments: It is quite evident from the survey that church discipline involves people's emotions. The emotions associated with church discipline are strong and frequent. For this reason it is especially important to exercise caution and restraint in administering discipline. Emotions can be used by God to elicit spiritual sensitivity and encourage healing. But the expression of undisciplined or uncontrolled emotions can result in division and disunity.

It is encouraging to see "restoration" and "healing" receive such high marks. Certainly these thoughts and feelings ought to be emphasized as pastors and elders lead their churches through the exercise of church discipline.

7. *In your experience, how frequently have these factors contributed to the neglect of church discipline?*

Anxious about personal confrontations: Often (2.93)
Lack of support by the congregation: Occasionally (2.43)
Lack of support by other leaders: Occasionally (2.26)
Lack of knowledge of procedures: Seldom (2.10)
Not wanting to give offense: Sometimes (2.71)
Not wanting to "pass judgment": Sometimes (2.70)
Concern for possible disunity: Often (2.79)
Fear of retaliation or lawsuit: Rarely (1.68)

Comments: It appears that Christian leaders have a difficult time putting their finger on the reason why church discipline is neglected. The highest mark (2.93) indicates that, of the factors listed, Christian leaders have the greatest concern over the matter of personal confrontation. That response might have been anticipated. Personal confrontation is frightening even for those with a good measure of self-confidence and conviction.

None of the options listed received significantly high marks. Perhaps many of the Christian leaders surveyed are simply not seeing church discipline as a biblical priority. They are busy with other ministries and responsibilities.

Concern about possible retaliation or lawsuits will probably increase as more and more churches are being sued in their attempts to exercise biblical church discipline. A California man has recently sued his church for five million dollars for slander and violation of counselor-counselee confidentiality. Concern for this issue will likely increase and, hopefully, lead church leaders to exercise caution in the administration of discipline rather than avoid it altogether.

8. *Consider the following activities and rate them as to the appropriateness of discipline:*

> Adultery: Almost always (3.65)
> Child abuse: Almost always (3.60)
> Wife beating: Almost always (3.56)
> Overeating: Seldom (1.90)
> Rebellious children: Seldom (2.12)
> Remarriage after divorce: Seldom (2.11)
> Homosexual activity: Frequently (3.43)
> Drunkenness: Frequently (3.27)
> Divorce: Occasionally (2.47)
> Incest: Always (3.76)
> Slander: Often (3.06)
> Heresy: Often (3.21)
> Anger: Seldom (2.22)
> Strife: Sometimes (2.54)
> Cheating: Often (3.08)
> Stealing: Frequently (3.43)
> Fornication: Frequently (3.48)
> Backbiting: Often (2.80)
> Abortion: Often (2.78)
> Covetousness: Occasionally (2.36)
> Drug Abuse: Often (3.18)

Comments: Some of the respondents had difficulty with this part of the survey. A Lutheran pastor who did not complete this section commented, "Each is conditional upon [the] situation." Another remarked that he could not make such evaluations "without taking it individual by individual." A Southern Baptist pastor stated, "Many of these depend on the individuals and circumstances."

Admittedly, the question was rather general. As a Conservative Baptist pastor explained, "This question is vague in that it doesn't specify what form the discipline should take." Another pastor responded, "My discipline would consist of private counseling and appropriate referrals for many of these." "It seems to me the key is not the sin, but the persistent unrepentant practice of the sin," remarked one pastor.

This question was designed to indicate whether some sins were considered more worthy of discipline than others. It was quite interesting that virtually all those surveyed indicated that *some* sins were more likely to necessitate church discipline than others. The sin which heads the list is "incest." "Adultery" comes in with a close second place. Next comes "child abuse" and "wife beating," with "fornication" and "homosexual activity" vying for fifth place.

It appears that we have yet to come to grips with the fact that sin is an *attitude* of rebellion against God which is manifested in various ways. Certainly all would agree that some sins have more serious consequences than others. But on the basis of our study, I would suggest that persistent sin, whatever the expression, is worthy of consideration for church discipline (cf. Gal. 6:1, "if a man is caught in *any* tresspass. . . .").

Abortion rated surprisingly low in terms of the appropriateness of church discipline. Of course there was quite a variety of views represented, from the United Methodists' (sometimes—2.59) to the Assemblies of God pastors' (frequently—3.42), with the Southern Baptists' somewhere in between (often—2.80). It was deemed more appropriate to discipline a church member for slander (3.06) than for abortion (2.78). Abortion remains a "hidden" and private issue in the minds of many Christians. Much work remains to be done in terms of educating the church about this most significant contemporary moral issue.

9. *On the scale of 1 to 4, rate the results which church discipline should be expected to achieve:*

> Turn others from similar sin: Often (2.99)
> Execute God's judgment on sin: Seldom (2.12)
> Restore the sinner to fellowship: Almost always (3.74)
> Bring about repentance: Almost always (3.72)
> Cause the sinner to leave the church: Almost never (1.49)
> Maintain a holy assembly: Often (2.92)

Comments: It is very encouraging to see the rather positive viewpoint regarding the results which church discipline should be expected to achieve. Rather than seeing church discipline as a means of punishment, the majority of pastors and Christian leaders view discipline as restorative—to bring about repentance and restore the sinner. This certainly reflects the view of Paul as evidenced by such passages as Gal. 6:1 and 2 Cor. 2:7–8.

10. *From your experience, identify the frequency of the following factors*

in contributing to the failure of church discipline:

> The offender refuses to repent: Often (2.93)
> The offender leaves the church: Often (2.94)
> Proper procedures are not followed: Sometimes (2.57)
> The church refuses to forgive: Occasionally (2.41)
> The church fails to restore: Sometimes (2.51)
> The offender transfers churches: Often (2.87)

Comments: The greatest difficulty in the exercise of church discipline appears to be the fact that the offender simply leaves the church or transfers churches. The problem is not corrected; it is simply transplanted. Thus church discipline is avoided. This action, of course, is the outworking of an attitude of unwillingness to repent. One pastor writes, ". . . in our denomination, persons whose lifestyle is incompatible with the Christian life tend to simply *drop out*." This is a serious problem. In order to be effective, the "drop out" loophole used to avoid church discipline must be closed.

For church membership to be meaningful, there must be a biblical sense of accountability in the relationship between pastor and parishioners, elders and people (cf. Heb. 13:17). This kind of accountability must be built into the church constitution. Since the relationship of membership is inaugurated on the basis of agreement and mutual consent, it would be reasonable to insist that the relationship of membership be terminated only with consent of the church members. This means that a church member who has "dropped out" is still part of the flock, though wayward. That sheep must be gently and lovingly coaxed back to the fold. That is what church discipline is all about—discipling the wayward Christian.

Reflecting on the Results

The survey has revealed that church discipline is not being totally ignored in America's churches. Many Christian leaders are seeking to administer biblical church discipline for the purpose of restoring sinning saints. While we aren't where we should be, we aren't as negligent in this matter as many might expect.

Several observations are particularly encouraging:
1. Most of those Christian leaders surveyed have participated in some form of church discipline.
2. Those surveyed generally viewed church discipline as restorative rather than punitive.

3. When discipline is applied, those surveyed enjoyed a measure of success in seeing restoration achieved.

Some observations indicate that we have a distance to go before the model of God's Word becomes the norm in His church:

1. We tend to discipline only the sins which are sexually objectionable and esthetically displeasing, while we ignore others.

2. The majority of Christian leaders view themselves as less than capable in dealing with situations which require discipline.

3. In almost half the cases where church discipline is administered, restoration fails to take place.

4. Saints in need of confrontation and correction are frequently allowed to slip away from the flock with little or no attempt made to retrieve them.

In 1 Thess. 4:10 the Apostle Paul commends the Thessalonian believers for their love of the brethren. Then he challenges them with these words: "But we urge you, brethren, to excel still more." This exhortation is quite appropriate for the matter of church discipline. The twentieth-century church in America is doing some things well. But there are some threads dangling, some tears that need mending. The third mark of the true church can be restored to American churches if Christian leaders will accept the challenge to "excel still more."

13
QUESTIONS CONCERNING CHURCH DISCIPLINE

The doctrine of church discipline has had nearly universal acceptance throughout the history of the Christian Church. Yet the teachings on this subject are often not applied. This is due in part to the objections raised against church discipline and the questions regarding its application. This chapter is designed to answer some of the major objections and questions on the church discipline issue.

1. *Didn't Jesus teach that we shouldn't judge others (Matt. 7:1–3)? This seems to argue against the principles of church discipline.*

What Jesus condemned in Matt. 7:1–3 was an attitude of judgmental criticism. The Pharisees were noted for their criticism of others. The problem was that their own closet wasn't clean (Matt. 23:13–36). Jesus is not suggesting that Christians ought not to be discerning (1 Cor. 14:19; 1 John 4:1). Nor is He suggesting that we ought to ignore the sins of a brother (Matt. 18:15; Luke 17:3). Jesus did not condemn all judgment. He did warn against a self-righteous, hypocritical attitude in judging others. To be discriminating is necessary; to be hypercritical is wrong.

Matt. 7:5 makes it clear that Jesus is not discouraging a proper evaluation of others. But He wants us to do so "with a clear eye." Understood in its context, Matt. 7:1–3 does not argue against the teachings on church discipline clearly presented by Jesus in Matt. 18:15–20.

2. *Doesn't the practice of church discipline encourage divisions and a "policeman" mentality for those in the church?*

Certainly it could. The key to avoiding this problem is the attitude with which the discipline is administered. The discipline of a sinning saint must be with a view to his restoration and done with a spirit of gentleness (Gal. 6:2). The offender is not to be treated as an enemy, but admonished as a brother (2 Thess. 3:15). If church discipline is carried out according to the teachings of the New Testament, divisions among members will be kept to a minimum. But even if difficulties should arise, I would agree with Daniel Wray that ". . . obedience to Christ and His Word is more important than an artificial 'unity' built on disobedience and compromise."[1]

3. *Jesus said to those accusing the adulterous woman, "He who is without sin among you, let him be the first to throw a stone at her" (John 8:7). How does this apply to the subject of church discipline?*

It is important to observe that Jesus does not condone the woman's sin. In fact, He appeals for her to make a clean break from sin (John 8:11). The incident illustrates Christ's mercy, compassion and willingness to forgive. There is no evidence that Jesus was "sweeping the issue under the rug." Jesus calls sin "sin." Yet He forgives. He grants forgiveness, not permission to sin.

Jesus' words in John 8:7 serve a dual purpose. They force the self-imposed judges to consider the attitudes of their own hearts. While outwardly innocent, they had no claim to sinlessness. Jesus' words also show the adulterous woman that there is hope. Though she was obviously guilty, Jesus offered her forgiveness and restoration. Like her accusers, Jesus acknowledged the woman's guilt. But unlike them, He viewed repentance and restoration as preferable to stoning.

We all have sinned and do not have the authority in and of ourselves to administer discipline. Yet Christ has given the church authority to administer discipline where sin persists without repentance. The incident in John 8 illustrates the attitude of gentleness necessary for the exercise of church discipline. It also exemplifies the objective—repentance and restoration.

4. *What does it mean to "deliver" someone "over to Satan" (1 Cor. 5:5, 1 Tim. 1:20)? Is this part of church discipline?*

Deliverance over to Satan is not a severe form of church discipline, but is virtually the equivalent of excommunication—the dismissal of an unrepentant offender from the church. This is evident from what Paul says in 1 Cor. 5:13: "Remove the wicked

---

[1]Daniel E. Wray, *Biblical Church Discipline* (Edinburgh: The Banner of Truth Trust, 1978), pp. 10–11.

man from among yourselves." To be removed from the church is to be delivered into the "domain of darkness" (Col. 1:13) where Satan holds sway (2 Cor. 4:4; 1 John 5:19). To live in Satan's realm is to be more vulnerable and exposed to his schemes. The purpose of such discipline is to cause the unrepentant sinner to recognize his need for Christ and His church and be restored (1 Cor. 5:5). Both Jesus and Paul instruct the church with regard to excommunication, the final step in church discipline (Matt. 18:17; 2 Thess. 3:14; Titus 3:10).

5. *How much time should be allowed between each step in the disciplinary process (Matt. 18:15–17)?*

This is an important issue, yet one that Jesus does not specifically address. Those who are closely involved in the disciplinary process must trust the leading of the Holy Spirit in making such decisions. Obviously, too much time will imply that repentance is not all that crucial. Too little time might result in procedures that tend to be more punitive than restorative. Ray Stedman, pastor at Peninsula Bible Church, emphasizes the importance of "ample time for repentance and change after each stage" of the disciplinary process. While "ample" might be considered vague, it implies that those directing the disciplinary process are spiritual leaders (Gal. 6:1) who are being led by the Holy Spirit in the decisions they make.

The chief criterion, suggests Wray, is the presence or absence of "*visible* progress, or *visible* responsiveness to admonition and rebuke."[2] If the offender is showing signs of softening as the Word of God is applied, time should be given for the Spirit of Christ to do His work (John 16:7–11). If after a reasonable time the offender demonstrates an unrepentant attitude or hardening of heart, then those involved in the disciplinary process would be wise to move to the next step.

6. *Why was Paul's rebuke of Peter in Gal. 2:11–14 public instead of private? Was Paul neglecting the proper steps in church discipline as outlined by Jesus (Matt. 18:15–17)?*

There are two possible explanations for Paul's public rebuke of Peter. First, it may be assumed, although not specifically stated in the biblical text, that Paul had already taken the initial steps in dealing with Peter. Perhaps Peter had failed to respond and Paul was now bringing the matter before the church. On the

---

[2]Ibid., p. 14.

other hand, there is evidence in 1 Tim. 5:20 that the sin of a church leader may require public rebuke regardless of any other circumstances or procedures. Those who sin are to be rebuked "in the presence of all" (cf. Gal. 2:14, 1 Tim. 5:20) that others may be fearful of the consequences of sinning. Either way the incident at Antioch is interpreted, it is unlikely that the Apostle Paul would be in conflict with Jesus on the procedures for church discipline.

7. *How can church discipline be accomplished without church membership? Should the church leaders attempt to discipline a person who is an "attender," but not a member?*

It is debated whether or not the early church actually had a membership roll. It seems likely that there was a recognized membership in the early church even though there may not have been a membership "roll" as many contemporary churches define it. The recognized members in the early church were those who had believed, been baptized, were sharing in the sacraments with the church family, and sitting under the instruction of the church leaders. It seems that from a scriptural point of view, there is little difference between a regular attender and a church member.

Church elders have spiritual responsibility for God's flock, and that includes regular attenders as well as church members (1 Pet. 5:2; Heb. 13:17). Hence it would be unwise to make any distinction between the two in the exercise of church discipline. Obviously it is not technically possible to excommunicate one who is not a church member. But that person can be corrected, rebuked and even disassociated from the church fellowship. The absence of official church membership is often an excuse for neglecting church discipline. It is quite unlikely that either Paul or Jesus would forego church discipline on such a mere technicality.

8. *When should church discipline be initiated? What sins are worthy of church discipline and which are not?*

Scripture does provide clear guidelines regarding what is acceptable for Christians and what is not. The sins identified in such listings as 1 Cor. 5:11; Gal. 5:19–21; Mark 7:21–22; and 2 Tim. 3:1–5 provide a tangible basis for beginning the exercise of church discipline. The use of such a list, however, may tend toward first-century Pharisaism. It also may suggest that as long as there is no outward manifestation of sin, one's spiritual life must be healthy. Only if a flagrant sin appears is it determined that something is wrong. Jeschke corrects this notion: "Where the signs of spiritual life are apparent, there is healthy Christian life. If these signs disappear, something is wrong. Then others in the church should come with help."[3]

According to the writer of Hebrews, the church leaders will give an account before God for their watchcare over the souls of God's flock (Heb. 13:17). This suggests that church leaders ought not to delay discipline until the sinner is in the last stages of spiritual abandonment. Don Bubna observes, "If we allow someone to grow distant from our fellowship without trying to find out why, there is little basis later for confrontation or healing."[4] Loving confrontation and correction should be initiated when the signs of a faltering faith first appear.

9. *Should the confession of a repentant sinner be made in public or in private?*

Confession is an important part of the process of restoration because it is one of the first evidences of genuine repentance. Certainly, confession must be made to God (1 John 1:9; Ps. 51:4). There are also times when confession should be made to other Christians (Matt. 5:23–24). There are two considerations which have bearing on whether such confession of sin should be public or private. First, who has been offended or sinned against? Second, who knows of the sin and needs to be aware of its consequences?

Those who have been offended, hurt or deceived by the sin must be aware that such transgression has been acknowledged and dealt with. It is impossible for restoration to fellowship to take place as long as there is some question as to whether sincere repentance has occurred.

In addition, those who know of the sin, although they might not have been personally hurt by it, need to know the matter has been fully and finally dealt with. James exhorts, "Therefore, confess your sins to one another, and pray for one another, so that you may be healed" (James 5:16). Public confession will impress on the minds and hearts of other Christians that even private sin has public consequences. Only a public confession will halt the rumor mill and stop wagging tongues. It must be again emphasized, however, that the purpose of any such confession is not to

---

[3]Marlin Jeschke, *Discipling the Brother* (Scottdale, Pa.: Herald Press, 1979), p. 187.
[4]Don Bubna, "Redemptive Love," *Leadership* 2 (Summer 1981), p. 80.

shame or humiliate, but to heal and restore.

10. *How detailed must the confession of a sinner be, especially when it is made in public?*

The confession should be detailed enough for those who have been offended, hurt or deceived to recognize the particular sin involved. It should be more than just the general statement, "I have sinned." Many Christians could say that about any day of the week! On the other hand, the confession should not provide unnecessary and unedifying details. It should not focus on the sensational or gruesome details of the offense committed. Paul says "it is disgraceful even to speak of the things which are done by them in secret" (Eph. 5:12).

It would be wise for the church leaders to discuss with the repentant offender the matter of public confession. They should agree beforehand on the procedures to be followed and the details to be revealed. There are some sins of the baser nature—homosexuality, incest, child molesting—which, in all honesty, are hard for people to understand and forgive. In *some* circumstances it may be best to avoid identifying the *particular* sin involved. Since public confession is with a view to restoration, caution should be exercised to avoid any hindrance to forgiveness, acceptance and reaffirmation.

11. *Should sinning saints be prohibited from participation when the Lord's Supper is observed?*

One of the most difficult problems Christians have wrestled with in the administration of church discipline is the relationship between excommunication and communion. Often suspension from participation in communion has been regarded as a step short of full excommunication. It is thought that a church member, because of unrepentant sin, may be forbidden the privilege of sharing in this most sacred act of Christian worship. The portion in 1 Cor. 5:11 ("[you are] not even to eat with such a one") is sometimes used to support such intermediate discipline before full excommunication.

In order to answer this question we must first have a proper understanding of the Lord's Supper. The communion table as instituted by our Lord is the sign of the New Covenant commemorating Christ's death and anticipating His second coming (Matt. 26:26–29; 1 Cor. 11:23–26). Concerning the Lord's Supper, Paul declares, "For as often as you eat this bread and drink the cup, you proclaim the Lord's death until He comes" (1 Cor.

11:26). Participation in the Lord's Supper is a "confessional act"[5] in which those participating declare to each other, and to the world, that they believe in the atoning death of Christ and are anticipating His second coming. It is an expression of personal faith and eschatological hope which can be made only by those in proper relationship with God; those who are enjoying both divine forgiveness and Christian fellowship.

One who is unqualified to participate in this confessional is in fact outside the circle of forgiveness and Christian fellowship. It would appear to be a contradiction to forbid participation in the Lord's Supper while at the same time permitting church membership to continue. This would seem to suggest that the church tolerates two levels of membership—the repentant and the unrepentant.

Rather than forbidding participation in the Lord's Table as a means of discipline, would it not be more biblical to use it as an instrument for discipleship? This is more in keeping with what Paul has to say in 1 Cor. 11:27–29 where he encourages careful self-examination so as to avoid participating in the Lord's Supper unworthily. Such self-examination and soul-searching will lead to repentance, confession, and then *participation* in the communion observance. As Paul says, "But let a man examine himself, and so let him eat of the bread and drink of the cup" (1 Cor. 11:28).

Preparation for communion ought to include opportunity for private meditation, public confession, and personal reconciliation with others. The Lord's Table should serve the church as a regular opportunity for each church member to have a spiritual check-up. Such preparation should be with a view to participation, not exclusion. As Jesus instructs, "If therefore you are presenting your offering at the altar, and there remember that your brother has something against you, leave your offering there before the altar, and go your way; first be reconciled to your brother, and then come and present your offering" (Matt. 5:23–24). The Lord's Supper is not an instrument of discipline; it is an opportunity for redisciplining those who have strayed from the way. The church family should be warned against unworthy or unrepentant participation in this observance and urged to make things right with God and man before sharing in this confessional act.

---

[5]Jeschke, *Discipling the Brother*, p. 107.

12. *What guidelines should be followed in a situation where an unrepentant excommunicated person continues attending church services? How should the church respond?*

No attempt should ever be made to forcibly evict an excommunicated church member from the pew. A church building is something of a public facility in the sense that visitors and guests (non-members) are on most occasions welcome. An "incident" involving the removal of an excommunicated member from the church would undoubtedly attract the attention of the press and could bring dishonor to Christ.

A better course of action would be to simply treat the excommunicated member as a non-member, but as a non-member under discipline. Certain kinds of social contact which involve the implication that "all is well" should be avoided. You would not want to invite the excommunicated to a Sunday school social, but you might sit down by the offender after church to discuss the necessity of repentance. The excommunicated should not be served communion nor should his or her "vote" or opinion be taken into consideration in any church business. Christians should avoid being unkind to an excommunicated member, but they should also avoid words and actions which may lead the offender to think that the sin has been forgiven and forgotten—without the requisite repentance.

13. *What sins in his past would prohibit a Christian from holding church office?*

This question actually involves two important issues—forgiveness and qualification for leadership. The Bible teaches that Christ forgives all sin on the basis of repentance and confession (1 John 1:9). To those who have entered into the New Covenant, God says, "I will forgive their iniquity, and their sin I will remember no more" (Jer. 31:34). Is it possible, then, for a believer to be completely forgiven and cleansed by the blood of Christ and still not be qualified for Christian leadership?

In Leviticus 21 God set forth stringent qualifications for Levites who would serve before the holy altar. A priest could not take a widow, former harlot or divorced woman as a wife. He could be disqualified by baldness, blindness, disfigurement or other physical defect. Such a priest could still eat of the offerings, but was disqualified from the ministry. The principle to be observed here is that God has very high standards for those who stand before Him as leaders of His spiritual community.

So too in 1 Tim. 3:1–7 Paul sets forth very high standards for those who aspire to the office of elder. Although saved, forgiven, and cleansed by the cross, not all Christians qualify for the office of elder. The elder must be "above reproach" and "have a good reputation with those outside the church" (1 Tim. 3:1, 7). These first and last qualifications are in the positions of emphasis and serve as an umbrella for the more specific qualifications in between.

As a general guideline, I would agree with Mark Littleton that past sin which has *continuing* ramifications would disqualify a believer from church leadership.[6] In time those ramifications may diminish in significance or be corrected. In such a situation, the Christian may at a future time be qualified for church leadership. Such decisions must be made with much prayer, biblical study and wise counsel. The church family should be in full agreement before any action is taken. It is unwise and spiritually unhealthy to thrust a person into a leadership position when there are serious questions among the membership regarding his qualification for ministry.

14. *To what extent should congregations cooperate in the matter of church discipline?*

Although there are many churches and denominations, there is one body of Christ. The unity of this body ought to be reflected in cooperation between churches seeking to restore sinning saints. Such cooperation may be necessary when a member about to be disciplined, or presently under discipline, transfers to another church. Frequently, unrepentant persons change churches in order to avoid discipline for matters they have been unwilling to correct. In such a situation, the receiving church is obligated to inquire about past church membership. It is quite appropriate in such cases to ask the former church about the circumstances of the transfer. The former church is obligated to state that the person in question did not leave the church in good standing and that there are some concerns which have not been resolved.

The former church must be very cautious, however, about disclosing any sins or offenses committed by the individual seeking transfer of membership. It would be best simply to state something like the following: "The church board must inform you that _____ is not a member in good standing at _____

---

[6]Mark R. Littleton, "Church Discipline: A Remedy for What Ails the Body," *Christianity Today* (May 8, 1981), p. 32.

Church. In view of his lack of repentance over some serious matters of personal conduct, we cannot recommend him to you for membership until such matters be resolved." To be more specific in identifying particular sins or offenses may incur the possibility of a lawsuit for invasion of privacy, as in the Marian Guinn case. If disciplinary steps have been taken, it would be well to mention that "_____ left _____ Church while under discipline."

Communication of this general nature alerts the receiving church to the problem, but leaves it with the responsibility of learning *from the erring saint* the particular offenses involved. The receiving church will then be encouraged, hopefully, to help him deal with these unresolved matters before being received into membership.

Another situation in which churches may find it helpful to cooperate in the matter of discipline would be where individuals from different churches are engaged in a conflict or are cooperating in a sin. In such circumstances it would be well to have representatives of the church boards meet with the individuals concerned and seek to resolve the problem—especially if it is a conflict. This joint committee could recommend disciplinary action if deemed necessary.

15. *How is discipline to be administered in the case of those who minister "outside" the church in para-church organizations?*

Every Christian ought to be a member of a local church where he can be under the oversight and spiritual watchcare of church elders (Heb. 10:25; 13:17). Consequently, those who minister in para-church organizations should be involved in local churches and be subject to discipline by the church and elders. In addition, some organizations, such as Jews for Jesus, have a "worker's agreement" which sets forth standards of the ministry and spells out the consequences of violating those standards.

Those ministering in para-church organizations have a dual accountability. They are accountable to their local church and to the organization they serve. In the case of an offense, discipline must be administered by the church. But the organization may take appropriate disciplinary steps as well. In certain cases the organization may find it necessary to limit or terminate the worker's ministry until genuine repentance can be demonstrated. This would be especially appropriate in the case of one who ministers to the Christian public at large like an author or nationally known speaker.

Both the church and the para-church organization would have a responsibility to seek restoration. While it would be preferable that the two work together in the process, this is not always practical. Churches and para-church organizations do not always agree on what steps are necessary to restore the worker to good standing. The church may be satisfied that genuine repentance has taken place. But the para-church may demand that certain criteria be met before the worker returns to public ministry. The standards may vary for the different roles or offices a Christian worker is involved in.

The problem arises, in some para-church organizations, when a leader becomes so powerful, authoritarian, and remote that he becomes responsible only to himself. There is no one to whom this leader must give an account. Consequently, if the leader commits a clear violation of integrity or spiritual leadership, no one feels it is his place to challenge, rebuke or discipline. Compromise and outright sin continue until public exposure brings shame and humiliation. This has been repeated time and time again.

Such problems might be avoided if every Christian leader would covenant with another Christian to be accountable to each other for their actions. Certainly, they should be accountable to their churches and organizational boards. But often churches view such leaders as remote and know little of their organizational ministry. And boards frequently become a mere "rubber stamp" for the plans and programs of the leader.

Personal accountability to a pastor friend has proven effective in my own life to help me avoid certain sins and temptations. I have told this special friend that if he sees a fault or sin in my life, he has an obligation to confront me. If I find myself stumbling into a sin, I have an obligation before the Lord to let him know. A planned program of mutual accountabilty may help some zealous Christian leaders avoid overstepping the bounds of ethics in the pursuit of their para-church ministries.

16. *If a Christian leader sins, then repents, when may he be restored to leadership? Who is responsible for this decision?*

When a Christian sins, repentance is the one prerequisite for forgiveness and restoration (Luke 17:3). However, in dealing with a leader, we must distinguish restoration to *fellowship* from restoration to *office*. Forgiveness of sin and restoration to fellowship take place immediately upon the basis of genuine repentance. (The genuineness of the repentance may be evidenced by confession of sin to those who have been offended or deceived.) Restoration to office and position of leadership may take time. The duration depends on the extent of the deception (Was he caught or did he confess?) and the seriousness of the sin.

Before a fallen leader can be restored to office, respect and trust must be restored. These qualities are associated with the requirement that the leader be "above reproach," "respectable," and "of good reputation" (1 Tim. 3:1–7). I am aware that these qualifications are given for one who aspires to the *office* of elder in the church. Yet I believe that one who *functions* as an elder in a Christian organization—exercising authority and oversight over Christian workers—should meet these basic biblical qualifications.

How long does it take to regain trust, respect and a good reputation after a serious moral fall? It may take as long as it took to earn it in the first place. But the "time" does not appear to be the crucial matter of consideration. What is crucial is that opportunity be given for the one seeking restoration to prove himself once again. This can be accomplished by giving responsibility at various levels, beginning with the lowest. As the repentant leader proves himself faithful in the accomplishment of those responsibilities, he can be advanced upwards. But beware of advancing the person beyond the point where he has the trust and respect of subordinates in the organization.

Who makes the decision as to when a fallen Christian leader is ready to be restored to office? In the context of the church, the elders (church board along with the pastoral staff) have responsibility for this decision (1 Tim. 5:17; Heb. 13:17). In churches with congregational polity, this could come to the church as a recommendation by the board. In Christian organizations, the officers or board must make the decision. In order to avoid internal conflict due to a lack of trust or respect for a former co-worker, it would be wise for the administrative officers or board to make such crucial decisions with counsel and input from the other workers in the organization.

17. *What place does the Holy Spirit have in the matter of church discipline?*

The Holy Spirit has a very important role in the administration of church discipline. First, it is the Holy Spirit that brings about a conviction of sin and stirs the offender to repentance.

Jesus said that the Holy Spirit would "convict the world concerning sin, and righteousness, and judgment" (John 16:8). While these words were spoken about the Holy Spirit's role in relationship to unbelievers, there is a definite application to the life of a backslidden saint. The Holy Spirit does a convicting work—awakening and proving guilt in the heart of the sinner.

Second, the Holy Spirit has an important role in illuminating the biblical teaching regarding church discipline. Jesus told his disciples that the Holy Spirit would "guide you into all the truth" (John 16:13). The Lord has given us a guide to church discipline—the Word of God. The Holy Spirit sheds light on the text giving us a proper understanding of these principles.

Third, the Holy Spirit will lead the church leaders and their congregations in the application of the biblical principles to particular situations. Paul declared in Romans 8:14 that those who are "being led by the Spirit of God, these are the sons of God." I am sometimes stumped by pastors who ask how to apply the principles of church discipline in an unusual or unique situation. I have often appealed to my life verse, Psalm 35:11, "They ask me things that I do not know." But I am confident that the Spirit of God will lead those responsible for the decision in applying the principles correctly.

18. *Is there a biblical answer for every question regarding the matter of church discipline?*

Many situations arise in the administration of church discipline for which there is no specific biblical command or "proof text." Yet we must not throw up our hands in despair. Jesus taught His disciples that the disciplinary actions of the church should be the result of unified opinion and fervent prayer (Matt. 18:19). And He promised that by His spiritual presence in the local assembly, the church's decision would be God's (Matt. 18:20). No, we don't have all the answers. But we have the abiding Christ who will help His people make the right decisions.

CONCLUSION:
CALLING THE CHURCH TO DISCIPLINE

Proclaiming the advantages of companionship, Solomon declares, "Two are better than one . . . for if either of them falls, the one will lift up his companion. But woe to the one who falls when there is not another to lift him up" (Eccles. 4:9, 10). The church this side of heaven is made up of saved people, some of whom will fall. As long as believers relax and let their hearts "grow cold," sin will inevitably occur until that glorious day when Christ welcomes His church home. Even leaders will fall. But woe to the one who falls where restorative church discipline is *not* practiced! For if the church neglects to lift up the fallen, who on earth will?

Church discipline is a biblical imperative. The church cannot neglect this imperative any more than it would willfully ignore Christ's commission to evangelize the nations. Church discipline is the corollary of evangelism. As evangelism reaches *out* to the unchurched, so church discipline reaches *in* to the redeemed community. Evangelism deals with sin in the lives of the unsaved. Church discipline deals with sin in the lives of those who have made professions of faith. Evangelism is the initial act of discipling whereas church discipline is part of the follow-up and shepherding of professing saints.

Can the church of the twentieth century afford to ignore this biblical imperative? The great Reformer, John Calvin, wrote strong words on this issue:

> . . . if no society, indeed, no house which has even a small family, can be kept in proper condition without discipline, it is much more necessary in the church, whose condition should be as ordered as possible. Accordingly, as the saving doctrine of Christ is the soul of the church, so does discipline serve as its

sinews, through which the members of the body hold together, each in its own place.

Calvin concludes his remarks with a stern warning:

> Therefore, all who desire to remove discipline or to hinder its restoration—whether they do this deliberately or out of ignorance—are surely contributing to the ultimate dissolution of the church.[1]

These words need to be taken into serious consideration by all who would choose by decision or default to neglect the biblical responsibility of confronting and correcting sinning saints.

In refocusing the church on the responsibility of discipline, it is necessary, first of all, to provide the people with solid, clear, biblical teaching on this matter. It is essential that we determine the scriptural procedures for church discipline before a crisis occurs. One pastor reported that he presented a series of sermons on church discipline every two years to continually educate his people on this subject. When teaching on church discipline, it is crucial to let the people know this isn't just the responsibility of the pastors and elders. It is the responsibility of the congregation as well. Paul referred to the discipline which was inflicted "by the majority" (2 Cor. 2:6). The church members have a responsibility to share in the process of discipline and restoration.

Christian leaders must not be intimidated by congregational resistance to the concept of church discipline. Careful exposition of the scriptural teaching on the subject will dissolve objections and prepare the way for this restoring and healing ministry. When circumstances require it, church discipline must be carried out in love with tears and sadness, not harsh pulpit-pounding. People resist a judgmental spirit but respond to a broken heart.

Someone has said, "Repetition with variety is the key to learning." In concluding this study it would be wise to briefly review the steps and procedures for church discipline. The following summary and "flow chart" will serve to guide Christians through the biblical steps of confronting and correcting sinning saints.

Initial Considerations

When you become aware of a sin in the life of a professing Christian, you as a brother or sister in Christ incur a biblical

---

[1]John Calvin, *Institutes of the Christian Religion*, 2 vols., ed. John T. McNeill (Philadelphia: The Westminster Press, 1960), pp. 1229–30 (Book IV, Chapter XII, Section 1).

responsibility to confront the offender. Pray for the person involved in the sin, for his responsiveness to the necessary confrontation. Deal first with your own sins and any bitterness or judgmental criticism in your heart. Two possible courses of action need be contemplated, depending on whether the offender is a church leader or a layman.

Steps for Discipline

The first step in any case where church discipline may be necessary is that of private confrontation. Don't speak to others about the sin; bathe your concern with prayer and then go directly to the offender. Tell the offender you value him too much to allow his sin not to be dealt with. Describe the sin and then give the person an opportunity to respond. Ask, "Is this true?" If the offender acknowledges the sin and displays repentance, move right into the process of forgiveness and restoration.

Of a leader

If the leader repents, restoration begins immediately. If the leader does not repent, it is necessary to bring forth witnesses who are able to vouch for the truth of the charges and assist in confronting the offender. Continued unrepentance would result in a public rebuke as an act of discipline. This would involve an announcement of the sin, its consequences, and the further consequences of lack of repentance. After giving the offender sufficient time to repent, the final step of discipline must be administered—excommunication and removal of ordination. This whole disciplinary process is with a view to repentance. If repentance occurs at any stage in the process, the steps for restoration should begin immediately.

Of a layman

If the offender refuses to acknowledge the sin in the face of reasonably strong evidence, or refuses to repent of admitted sin, confront the person a second time in the company of two or three witnesses. It is not necessary for them to have actually witnessed the act of sin. Yet they should be able to cite evidence against the offender in hopes of turning the brother or sister back to God. If the sin is acknowledged, the process of restoration must begin.

If the offender refuses to repent in response to personal confrontation in private, the whole church must be brought into the disciplinary process. The offense must be announced to the church members so that they as a congregation may exert their influence and intercession for the purposes of repentance. This must be done discreetly and with loving concern for the offender. In taking this significant step, it would be well to remember that the ultimate objective is *restoration*. Bridges of relationship must be maintained in order to draw a repentant sinner back into the church fellowship. If the sinner repents, the steps for restoration must commence.

If the person refuses to repent in response to congregational discipline, it becomes necessary to disfellowship him from the church. Since he is acting as an unbeliever, he must be treated as one. This means you continue to minister to the offender, but as you would to an unsaved person, not as a fellow-believer.

Steps for Restoration

Restoration to fellowship with Christ and His church is the ultimate goal of any act of church discipline. The condition for restoration is genuine repentance from sin. Genuine repentance can be evidenced by the fruits of confession: sorrow for sin, acceptance of its consequences, willingness to make restitution for a wrong done, and avoidance of such sin in the future.

Of a leader

The first step in the process would be a public acknowledgment of the sin and its consquences so that "all may fear" and be deterred from transgression. This step, which compares to the "public rebuke" in the case of the unrepentant leader, would include an acknowledgment of the offence and a report that repentance has taken place. The leader must then begin the long process of restoring relationships with those who were deceived or sinned against. When trust, credibility and reputation are renewed, the fallen leader may be restored to a position of ministry or church office.

Of a layman

The restoration of a layman focuses on the relationship he has with God's people. When repentance has been evidenced, complete forgiveness must be expressed by those who have been offended. This may involve a statement by the church, by individuals or both. Those who have forgiven the offender then have the Christian duty to comfort the repentant sinner and reaffirm Christian love. This will prevent Satan from taking advantage of a bitterness which may rise when forgiveness is neglected.

The church of Christ must maintain biblical discipline or be held in contempt both by those who love righteousness and those who promote evil. The exercise of biblical church discipline requires much courage, great wisdom and spiritual sensitivity. Thorough study and diligent prayer is needed to prepare the way for biblical discipline to be restored and reemphasized in our churches. The task before us is great, but not impossible. A willingness to submit to the teachings of Christ is the key to the accomplishment of this goal. Nearly two thousand years ago Jesus asked the probing question, "Why do you call Me, 'Lord, Lord,' and do not what I say?" (Luke 6:46). Is He still asking "why"?

CHURCH DISCIPLINE FLOW CHART

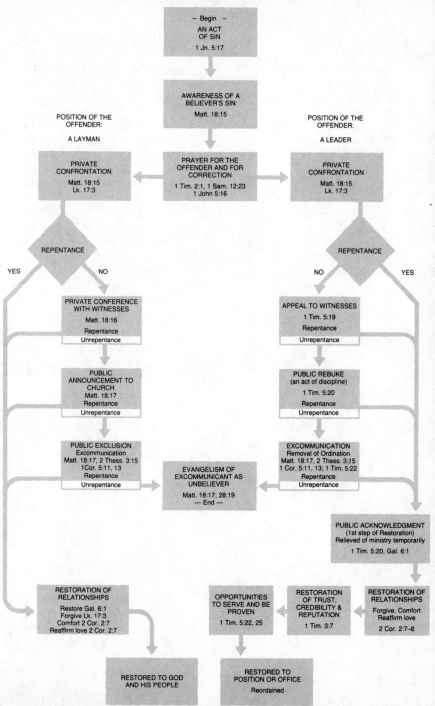

SELECTED BIBLIOGRAPHY

Augsburger, David. *Caring Enough to Confront*. Glendale, Calif.: Regal Books Division, G/L Publications, 1973.

Baker, Don. *Beyond Forgiveness*. Portland: Multnomah Press, 1984.

Bubna, Donald L. "Redemptive Love: The Key to Church Discipline." *Leadership* 2 (Summer 1981): 77–85.

Buzzard, Lynn R. and Eck, Laurence. *Tell It to the Church*. Elgin, Ill.: David C. Cook Publishing Co., 1982.

Burge, Joan. "The Church that Dares to Discipline." *Christian Life* (August 1980): 26–47.

Engle, Paul E. "When It's Okay to Pass Judgment." *Moody Monthly* (May 1981): 37–39.

Gage, Ken and Joy. *Restoring Fellowship: Judgment and Church Discipline*. Chicago: Moody Press, 1984.

Heideman, Gene P. "Discipline and Identity." *Reformed Review* 35 (Fall 1981): 17–25.

Knuteson, Roy E. *Calling the Church to Discipline*. Nashville: Action Press, 1977.

Jeschke, Marlin. *Discipling The Brother*. Scottdale, Pa.: Herald Press, 1972.

Lines, Neil M. "Church Discipline: Ruination or Restoration." D.Min. product, Western Conservative Baptist Seminary, 1982.

Littleton, Mark R. "Church Discipline: A Remedy for What Ails the Body." *Christianity Today* (May 8, 1981): 30–33.

Lutzer, Erwin W. "Restoring the Fallen." *Moody Monthly* (June 1984): 106–107.

Megillian, Keith. "The Ministry of Rebuking." *Journal of Pastoral Practice* 5 (1981): 22–25.

Oberholzer, Emil. *Delinquent Saints*. New York: AMS Press, Inc., 1968.

Palau, Luis. "Discipline in the Church." *Discipleship Journal* (issue 16, 1983): 16–20.

Walker, Warham. *Harmony in the Church*. Rochester, N.Y.: Backus Book Publishers, 1981.

Wiersbe, Warren. "When My Brother Sins." *Moody Monthly* (February 1983): 95–99.

Wray, Daniel E. *Biblical Church Discipline*. Edinburgh: The Banner of Truth Trust, 1978.

SUBJECT INDEX

172

SCRIPTURE INDEX